Advance Reviews

The perfect primer for the newbie, the required reference resource for the pro—if you're a product manager, you must have this book.
—Cliff Conneighton, Chairman
Marketing Roundtable
Author, *Venture Management Handbook*

This book gets right to the point in helping product managers of smaller software companies understand what they need to do, when they need to do it, and how, to get their jobs done. It also lays the foundation for their professional development as they enable their companies to achieve marketplace success.
—Steven Haines, Founder and President
Sequent Learning Networks

Software Product Management Essentials is a "Must Read" for anyone in their first few years of product management. Given the lack of formal training most Product Managers receive, it is an excellent resource for learning what you need in order to be successful. We recommend it to many of the Product Managers at our client companies."
—Brian Lawley
President & Founder, **The 280 Group**
President, **Silicon Valley Product Management Association**

The job of product management often appears overwhelming. Alyssa Dver's book helps the new product manager know where to begin and gives specific tools to make the new product manager productive quickly. Designed for small to mid-sized companies, Dver introduces the broad scope of product management in an easily readable format. The book also provides the most commonly used templates so that readers will not have to "reinvent the wheel." *Software Product Management Essentials* is filled with practical advice from an author who has clearly succeeded in the job.
—Steve Johnson
Pragmatic Marketing (www.pragmaticmarketing.com)

This book very nicely bridges the gap between the important principles of product management and the very essential day-to-day tasks that practicing software product managers must accomplish.
—Shimon Shmueli, President
Washington DC Chapter of PDMA

Dver makes it abundantly clear to her target readers that the path to market leadership begins with product management. The book gives product managers a great perspective on the persona, skills, and bandwidth required to keep the product management function in a leadership position within the organization.
—John Mansour, President
ZIGZAG Marketing

In a crucial business and technical area such as Product Management, it is imperative that there are quality resources such as the book, *Software Product Management Essentials*. The book is an easy to read, hands-on look at the activities involved in being a successful product manager. Readers will truly appreciate the wisdom in the book to help make them efficient and effective. This is a must-read for any software product manager, new and old, who wants to ensure that they are doing the best possible job.
—Jacques Murphy, Editor
Product Management Challenges Newsletter

Alyssa Dver's new book, *Software Product Management Essentials*, is a long-overdue compendium on one of the most important and misunderstood functions within any technology company. When JTBN adds Special Interest Groups (SIGs) this should be required reading for everyone regardless of functional area. Colleges should take note and offer a course based on this pragmatic book.
—Barbara Finer, Founder HTMP, Executive Committee
JTBN (Jewish Technology Business Network)

Software Product Management Essentials

Software Product Management Essentials

A practical guide for small and mid-sized companies

Alyssa S. Dver

2007 Anniversary Printing
Includes:
The 7 Habits of Highly Effective Product Managers
Web 2.0 Topics: Blogs, Podcasts, Wikis, Screencasts and more.

Anclote Press
Tampa, Florida, USA
www.anclote.com
Publishers of Actionable Information for the 21st Century

Publisher's Cataloging-in-Publication Data

Dver, Alyssa.
Software Product Management Essentials.
  p. cm.
    Includes appendices and index.
    ISBN 0-929652-01-0 (paperback : alk. paper)

    1. Product management 2. Computer software - Marketing. 3. Computer Software Industry - Marketing. 4. New products - Marketing. I. Dver, Alyssa. II Title

HF5439.C67 D84 2003   2003104527
005.3'068'8–dc21 Dver   CIP

Book's Web site: http://www.anclote.com/dver.html
Cover design by Tad Fingar

Published by Anclote Press
An Imprint of Meghan-Kiffer Press
310 East Fern Street — Suite G
Tampa, FL 33604 USA

Company and product names mentioned herein are the trademarks or registered trademarks of their respective owners.

Anclote Press books are available at special quantity discounts for corporate education and training use. For more information write Special Sales, Anclote Press, Suite G, 310 East Fern Street, Tampa, Florida 33604 or call (813) 251-5531.

Anclote Press
Tampa, Florida, USA
Publishers of Actionable Information for the 21st Century
Printed in the United States of America.   SAN 249-7980
Anclote Printing   10 9 8 7 6 5

This book is dedicated to all those brave individuals who are or think they may want to be software Product Managers. May this book be a source of great inspiration and support. A special acknowledgment to Steve Zagame who so willingly introduced me to global Product Management and to Marco Emrich who has been and continues to be my mentor. Thank you to my family members for their unconditional support.

Table of Contents

Introduction

Product Management is one of the most attractive career paths available in any type of company, particularly software organizations. Recruiters confirm that experienced Product Managers, at any level, possess one of the most challenging skill sets to find. Yet, despite the demand for top Product Management talent, few available resources focus on this job function. A study of sales and marketing executives by consulting group Sirius Decisions found that executives feel that the core competency needing most improvement in their organizations is indeed, product management. Most product management books and classes teach high-level concepts dealing with all kinds of products, from baby diapers to software packages, without acknowledging the differences in managing them. While there are indeed similarities at a high level, the details and tactical implementation strategies are vastly different and new *software* Product Managers find little support for the overwhelming tasks ahead of them.

This book focuses on smaller companies with less than 100 employees. With fewer resources to rely on, Product Managers in smaller companies must do many tactical things themselves, in addition to managing the product strategy and overall delivery process. The bigger the organization, the more people the Product Manager (PM) needs to coordinate, but bigger organizations can also offer more help to the PM in addressing the multitude of tasks required.

This book represents more than 20 years of hands-on experience and research in large, medium and small organizations, that can help guide new PMs along their journey. It reveals some best practices that are best-kept secrets of the software industry. In working at different companies and interviewing dozens more, I have discovered consistent processes that make the job of Product Manager less dependent on trial and error. This book describes these practices and provides advice to keep PMs on track as they manage their products throughout the product lifecycles.

In small companies where everyone wears "many hats," the Product Manager participates in every aspect of product development—from engineering to marketing, finance and sales. In fact, these lines are blurred as the PM *champions* the product throughout its lifecycle, working intimately with each functional group in the company to ensure the best possible delivery and support of the product. Because the PM can be easily overwhelmed by trying to take on too much, the book provides guidance especially useful to PMs in small and mid-sized software companies. It provides means to prioritize work in order to complete what must be accomplished by the PM or others in the organization. Regardless of the structure and size of the organization, the PM will often manage conflicting priorities and decide how to best interact with others involved in the product delivery process.

Product management is anything but simple because it is laden with apparent contradictions. Product Managers have accountability for the success of the product but rarely have direct line authority. Therefore they must "influence" rather than "manage." To be credible, PMs must be the experts and know more about their products and markets than anyone, yet they also must continuously strive to gather input from all parties in their quests to remain experts and to be impartial judges of requirements. This book is dedicated to providing relief to PMs faced with this formidable (and sometimes seemingly impossible) challenge

The book discusses the key issues facing a software PM and presents very specific processes and protocols for organizing and managing the people and deliverables needed to make sure that software product are delivered to market on time, with outstanding quality. The information and templates in this book provide starting points to develop processes and documents that will work for any organization. There is no one "right set of processes" that guarantees success, but this book describes approaches that have been proven to work in a cross-section of software companies. The information, templates and approach of this book can be customized to fit any company's specific needs.

Product Managers have a very important job and one that the entire company counts on. Because the responsibilities of a PM can seem boundless and there is always more to do, they become a master of prioritizing tasks as well as deploying processes that keep the company organized and efficient. This book provides the tools needed to be a recognized great Product Manager and a true champion of software products.

Product Champion

Chapter 1:
What is Product Management?

Many professional job titles are vague, but few are as variable as that of the "Product Manager". Even within the software industry, the definition and role of the Product Manager varies widely. In some companies Product Managers are responsible for managing the brand of the product or the entire marketing mix including lead generation and sales support. Other companies locate brand management as a separate function within corporate marketing. Some companies view Product Managers as the liaison between sales and engineering, helping to define and refine product requirements and specifications. In yet other companies the Product Manager is the business manager for a product or a product group. As a result, it is difficult to pinpoint a definitive role across the board for the Product Manager.

Regardless of the exact definition of role of the Product Manager, this book is designed to meet the needs of the small and mid-sized software companies that typically have one hallmark product. In such firms, the entire company is responsible for the success of "the product" but the Product Manager's role stands out as one of product *champion*. In a small company, the business plan typically revolves around a single product or technology. The plan is written by the executive team and in many cases developed as part of the start-up work needed to raise initial capital and attract key employees. The Product Manager is rarely the author or owner of the business plan, for it represents the entire business and the roles and responsibilities of everyone in the firm. In start-up companies, the hallmark product is likely decided, researched, and documented as part of the business plan to prove viability and forecasted opportunity. After this is determined, the Product Manager may be responsible for keeping the product-specific parts of the plan updated, and developing additional tactical plans such as a Product

Business Plan (PBP), discussed in Chapter 4. While there is some noticeable overlap with a company's overall business plan, the PBP elaborates the tactical details of the product and its delivery. It is an internal document used to record and share critical product information. The overall company business plan is typically used for external audiences to help raise money and foster business relationships since it emphasizes company financial and strategic plans.

Once a software company decides what product to make, the Product Manager's responsibility is to manage the overall product delivery process and champion the product and its benefits to many audiences, including the press, analysts, customers, prospects, employees, the Board of Directors and other stakeholders. The PM must present the product in the most attractive way for the specific audience, and therefore the position requires a unique combination of communication skills along with business and technical knowledge. To be successful, the Product Manager must have credibility and subsequent influence over the product's strategic direction and development process. To do this, a Product Manager must have the knowledge and communication skills to lead and be trusted by a variety of personalities, including engineers and customers. By owning processes such as product requirements and product delivery, Product Managers become repositories of critical information, and will remain intimately involved with all aspects of the product throughout its lifecycle.

The PM is directly involved with pricing decisions, product positioning and pre- and post-sales support. The PM's responsibilities demand deep product knowledge—why and how the product was conceived, how it is currently being used, and what direction it is going. The PM must be an overall product expert and the person at the center of the business activities that surround the product throughout its lifecycle. Indeed, the Product Manager is the person who probably gets the most email in the company!

The role of the Product Manager is often confused with that of the "Product Marketing Manager" (PMM). While these roles and responsibilities may be intertwined, the Product Manager typically works more closely with engineering throughout the product lifecycle and is responsible for the overall product delivery process, which will involve marketing. If both roles are present in a given company, the Product Manager works with the Product Marketing Manager to develop positioning based on the research and overall information available about the product and its market. The Product Marketing Manager, in turn, focuses on communicating product information to outside audiences. The consulting company, Pragmatic Marketing, provides a useful distinction: "A PM listens to the market; a PMM talks to the market." From its 2002 survey, Pragmatic Marketing reported the following comparisons:

	PM Percent	PMM Percent
Preparing business case	53.70%	44.90%
Researching market needs	73.10%	78.70%
Writing requirements	81.20%	51.20%
Writing detailed specifications	34.30%	14.20%
Monitoring development projects	85.40%	44.10%
Writing copy for promotional material	35.60%	69.30%
Approving promotional material	51.80%	65.40%
Training Sales people	49.80%	62.20%
Going on sales calls	34.60%	40.90%
Performing win/loss analysis	14.60%	21.30%

To be a good Product Manager, a solid blend of technological and business acumen is required. To be a great PM, outstanding oral and written communications are essential, in conjunction with confidence, a general "whatever it takes" attitude and pride in one's product.

One criterion used to judge the effectiveness of a PM is the quality of the PM's product knowledge. Having product knowledge means a deep understanding of how the product works, how customers use it, what the competition offers, and how competitors' products differ. The PM need not know the lines of software code inside the product, but must know the technology and techniques used to build the code, the industry standards that are supported, and the prerequisite products and knowledge needed to use the product. The PM must understand why the product was created to begin with, what specific problems it solves, the scope of the problem that the product is targeting, and the product capabilities and limitations. In order to establish oneself as "the" product champion, the PM should use the product if possible, as well as talk to other active users of the product on an ongoing basis. In direct terms, *the more a Product Manager knows about the target market, the applicability of the product versus other solutions, and specifically how the product is used, the more effective (s)he will be as a Product Manager.*

The PM must be able to paint the vision for the product in terms of what it can do today and what it will be able to do in the future. The Product Manager must carry the flag for the product and build a market perception about its capabilities and position alongside the competition. One of the challenges of the PM is balancing what the market perceives that the product can do, versus what it actually can do. Product Management is as much about sales and marketing (internal and external) as it is about process and delivery. Developing and managing product expectations involves positioning and promotion, in addition to actual product capabilities.

Product Managers must multi-task and therefore they must be experts in managing priorities and staying organized. Beyond marketing, sales, support or other such functions, PMs must be able to juggle many tasks and make careful decisions about those they need to delegate. In some cases, tasks that are not essential will need to be weeded out in light of critical activities that must be accomplished. Product Management is not for the perfectionist or the negativist, the hardcore engineers or highly creative marketers. These functions are, however, frequent breeding grounds for Product Managers. One could argue that Product Managers are, in truth, a breed of their own.

Product Management is sometimes a thankless job. The PM is the first to know when there is a problem, the first to be held accountable for overall product decisions, and the first to blame when sales can't make quota because the product is missing functionality. However, being in the center of the business can be a tremendously rewarding opportunity, and the skills learned as a PM can be leveraged in most any other career path. Many companies recognize that product management as the ideal training ground for future presidents. For the right person, the challenges and rewards of being a Product Manager can command an entire career.

Profile of a Product Manager

Taken from a Pragmatic Marketing 2005 survey of 484 respondents:

✓ The average Product Manager is:
  - 36 years old
  - 87% claim to be "somewhat" or "very" technical
  - 90% have completed college, 46% have some MBA classes and 40% have completed a masters program
  - 33% are female, 67% are male.

✓ The typical Product Manager has responsibility for three products.

✓ The typical Product Manager reports to a director in the Marketing department.
  - 46% report to a director
  - 28% to VP
  - 15% are in the Marketing department
  - 5% report to the CEO
  - 21% are in the Product Management department
  - 12% are in Development or Engineering
  - 5% are in a Sales department

✓ Product Managers receive 50 emails a day and send about 25.

✓ On average, they attend 15 meetings each week, but 27% are attend more than 20 meetings!

✓ The majority of Product Managers are researching market needs, writing requirements and monitoring development projects.
  - 66% researching market needs
  - 54% preparing business case
  - 77% writing requirements
  - 52% writing specifications
  - 79% monitoring development projects

✓ Product Managers still spend a lot of time providing technical content for marketing communication (MarCom) and sales.
  - 49% writing promotional copy
  - 47% approving promotional materials

- 51% training Sales people
- 44% going on sales calls
- 23% creating web content

Sample Product Manager Job Descriptions

Sample #1

As Product Manager, you will guide a team that is charged with a product line contribution as a business unit. This extends from increasing the profitability of existing products to developing new products for the company. You will build products from existing ideas, and help to develop new ideas based on your industry experience and your contact with customers and prospects. You must possess a unique blend of business and technical savvy, a big-picture vision, and the drive to make that vision a reality. You must enjoy spending time in the market to understand customer problems, and find innovative solutions for the broader market.

You must be able to communicate with all areas of the company. You will work with an engineering counterpart to define product release requirements. You will work with marketing communications to define the go-to-market strategy, helping them understand the product positioning, key benefits and target customer. You will also serve as the internal and external evangelist for your product offering, occasionally working with the sales channel and key customers.

KEY RESPONSIBILITIES
- Managing the entire product line life cycle from strategic planning to tactical activities
- Specifying marketing requirements for current and future products by conducting market research supported by ongoing visits to customers and non-customers
- Driving a solution set across development teams (primarily development, engineering and marketing communications)

through market requirements, product contract and positioning
- Developing and implementing a company-wide go-to-market plan, working with all departments to execute
- Analyzing potential partner relationships for the product along with business development

REQUIREMENTS
- 3+ years of software marketing/product management experience
- Knowledgeable in technology
- Computer science or engineering degree or work experience a strong plus
- This position requires travel to customer and non-customer sites in North America and Europe (25%)

Excerpted from Pragmatic Marketing's Website: www.productmarketing.com

Sample #2

Product management or demonstrated ability to produce detailed user requirements, work with developers to determine detailed product requirements and designs, and create product roll-out materials. Needs to have experience with enterprise software that may include: workflow and document management, asset planning and tracking, project management including financial components, decision support, BPM, et al. As part of this role is ensuring the product suite interfaces with 3rd party software and systems, experience with API's and integration (especially from a project management perspective) is highly desirable. Specific domain expertise not required.

- Team with sales, service, marketing, product development and product management to define, develop, market, sell and deliver the product and the product value proposition.
- Translate market needs into clearly defined and detailed product user requirements. Provide regular and detailed communications of product and market status and changes.

- Partner with product development to communicate product requirements and determine viable development strategies, deliverables, and release dates.
- Evaluate competitive market offerings and deliver on differentiation and analysis studies, positioning and communications.
- Team with product marketing, product development, sales and service to oversee and shepherd the product (or components) through the Phase Review Lifecycle.
- Provide product specific support to sales, marketing, professional services and training teams.

Sample #3:

Position Overview

This position is responsible for making sure the right product gets delivered on time with acceptable quality. The Product Manager works closely with the Product Marketing Manager to define release strategy and content. The successful candidate will manage the product release process from definition through delivery and on-going maintenance and will be responsible for coordinating the cross-functional activities involved in product development and release.

General Responsibilities:

- Working with Product Marketing to define release strategy and content
- Working with customers, product marketing, sales, support and engineering to gather input for product requirements
- Writing detailed product requirements and obtaining cross-functional sign-off
- Managing the product release process from definition through delivery and ongoing maintenance

- Coordinating cross-functional teams to ensure a smooth rollout
- Defining and managing the beta test and early release programs
- Balancing time to market and quality requirements to decide when the product is ready for release

Educational Requirements:

- BS in Computer Science, or BA in Business Management
- Coursework in engineering or a background in technical roles within application software environment a plus

Required Experience:

- 6-9 years product management experience for enterprise level software applications
- Strong, proven experience in managing product requirements and product release planning
- Experience in the pharmaceutical industry, particularly drug safety is highly desirable
- Excellent team and project management skills
- Excellent verbal and written communication skills
- Travel is required with some international visits

The 7 Habits of Highly Effective Product Managers

Product management is the most contradicting of all professions. Product Managers (PMs) need to be product experts and perpetual students. They are accountable for the business with the only tool of influence. They must be creative, articulate multimedia marketers, able to speak the technology, finance, and legalese. No wonder there are so few great Product Managers.

After 20 years researching and working with all types of Product Managers, it is evident what distinguishes a good Product Manager from a great one. Here I boil it down to 7 key attributes:

1. Great Product Managers know their product but also knows their own limits.

Obviously, a PM needs to know as much about the product as possible including the customers and their use of the product, the competition, the pricing, and so on. It doesn't mean that the PM should know the details of the code or database schema. Nothing ticks off engineers like a know-it-all PM. Yes, the PM should be aware of the overall architecture, what language or toolkit was used, any standards supported, and interoperability requirements. However, leave the development details to the pros. A PM will be more respected for it.

2. A great Product Manager listens first.

A PM's job is to evangelize but the biggest failure in doing this is to assume too much about your audience. Engage and educate people by listening to them first. A great PM will find out specifically what their audience wants to know and the best way to deliver it.

3. Great Product Managers ask why, not what.

Great PMs know not to jump on every suggestion made for a product enhancement or pricing adjustment. They ask why the change is important before expending valuable time and resources. Only the answers to "why" can expose if there is already a less obvious solution or if there are other ways to address the opportunity.

4. Great Product Managers are decisive.

PMs must make decisions regularly and as such, they should be firm and ready to defend their decisions. Great PMs get data when it's available and if not, they acknowledge that it is the best decision under the circumstances. They also are prepared to change their decision if more information becomes available and the change is yet positive.

5. Great Product Managers are responsive.

It is necessary to let people know that you aren't ignoring them. When unresponsive, people assume you are unorganized, pretentious, or incapable. Great PMs are conscientious about their own image and reputation as they are about their product's.

6. Great Product Managers communicate frequently, concretely and concisely.

The hardest talent may be to say a lot with only a few words. A great way to do this is to use charts, graphs, and other pictorial representation of complex information. Another way is to spend time becoming a great writer and speaker. These are not natural gifts but rather practiced arts which when mastered, are the means to gain and sustain attention and credibility.

7. Great PMs manage confident passion

Passion is critical and can't be faked. However, too much passion is annoying. Great PMS are enthusiastic but they don't lose an honest perspective that not everyone agrees that their baby is beautiful. Great PMs never lose their temper at a colleague or superior. They are the ever level-headed negotiators and influencers. Their opinions are strong but they also strive to obtain win-win. This is an art form as much as it is a personality trait but great PMs have the confidence to do the right thing and do it with style.

Chapter 2:
The Development Process

While the software code is only one aspect of your total product, the software is obviously the critical part. A clean, efficient software development process is key to delivering quality software on time. Every software company needs a formal development process. The development process is where the software product begins and ends. Some of the more popular development processes are: Agile Software Modeling Development, eXtreme Programming (XP), Unified Software Development Programming, Scrum, Crystal Light, Feature Driven Development (FDD), and Dynamic System Development Method (DSDM). While there are dozens of books are dedicated to these specific development processes, this chapter presents guidelines for selecting a development process that's right for any one organization's specific product delivery needs. One example development process, The Base Level Integration Process (BLIP), is highlighted here. The BLIP process has been proven successful for several small software organizations. It is described in detail for the purposes of understanding what is involved in a software development process and how it works.

A successful process helps drive action and accountability, and when used effectively, provides a tool for continuous process improvement, driving quality up and time to release down—the keys to overall competitiveness. The implementation of proven engineering processes can help sell the product as it demonstrates discipline and a sense of urgency that is reflected in the company image that is portrayed to the market.

Selecting a Development Process

When selecting and implementing a development process, it is imperative to have consensus on which process that the organization will use and stick to—from the top to the bottom of the organization. As with any process, a lack of commitment is the real productivity killer. Good processes ensure organization alignment, reliability and the continuous improvement of activities throughout the journey. Because software development is one of the most complex of human endeavors, unless the organization is willing to commit to a solid development process and provide the necessary resources needed for continuous improvement, success will only be an accidental outcome.

Software development requires tradeoffs. When considering what and how the product will be developed or enhanced, decide on the relative priorities of quality, functionality and time.

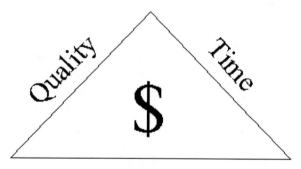

Functionality/Performance

The Software Development Triangle

Ideally all products will have the highest quality, the most functionality, with superb performance and be delivered on time. On the other hand, every product is bounded by these three constraints and the challenge is to achieve the ultimate goal of all three, profitably. We must balance the variables due to cost tradeoffs, as additional resources are needed to increase the quality, functionality or timeliness of the product. These additional resources (costs) can sometimes exceed the anticipated revenue benefits. While there should always be goals set for each aspect, limited resources will force any company to make hard decisions as to what is enough. Even the world's best-known software companies produce what analysts call "good-enough" software. One of the greatest challenges of the Product Manager is to maintain a balance here.

Answers to three key questions can help determine which development process is most appropriate.

1. How often does the organization need or want to release software to the market? This will be influenced by the complexity of the product as well as the number of installations expected. A mass-market product, for example, will have a higher demand for regular releases that include a handful of new features. Most web applications are frequently updated with minimal disruption to the users. These types of customers expect that bug fixes and other maintenance patches will be released as they are available. Typically installing a maintenance patch is not a big problem and users of the product can do this on their own. Larger system implementations, however, may not be this flexible and so may have only one or two releases per year that may require the company's technicians to install the product and do quality assurance (QA) at the customer's site.

Another important release frequency barometer is the rate at which customers can absorb new software. In some organizations, especially smaller ones, many users may lack a convincing need or lack the technical support to upgrade their systems regularly. For these customers, new releases must be planned well in advance and justified against other business needs.

Determine the release frequency that is most appropriate for the product. Some development processes are designed for longer time periods between releases, while others are designed for more rapid cycles. Some rely on the use of rapid development and prototyping (spiral lifecycle) while others require large amounts of documentation and specification before a single line of code is written (a waterfall model). Knowing the desired release frequency of a product will determine the appropriate lifecycle model.

Spiral Life-Cycle

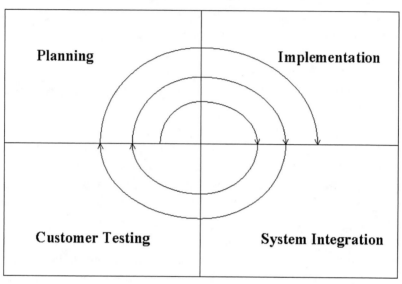

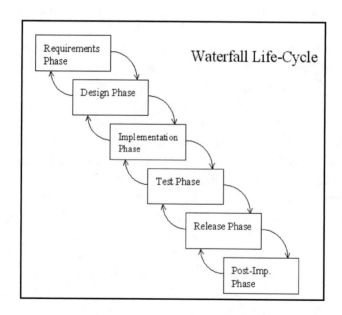

2. How much administration is required by the process and does the company have the appropriate administrative resources available? Some development processes or complementary quality processes (e.g. ISO 9000/9001/9002, Total Quality Management (TQM) and Six Sigma) may require extensive documentation and monitoring. Smaller software companies cannot afford to support separate quality staff and must carefully craft a strategy to use available resources to incorporate such essential quality processes.

3. Which attribute (quality, functionality, time) is the most important? Ensure that the development process will allow the company to focus on that aspect. Each development process must account for all three sides of the triangle, but they typically excel in one or two. Select a development process that is flexible enough to allow the organization to select which attribute is the priority from one release cycle to the next. Although tradeoffs must be made, one attribute for another, be sure the tradeoffs are made consciously. For example, if the company wants to be the leader in quality, the development process must dedicate enough time and resources to that aspect of the cycle. If new features will be the key to success, look for a process that supports prototyping and rapid development. Time-to-market could also be the driving criterion that can make or break a product. Most software development processes respect all three attributes but may need to be adjusted to accommodate time and resource constraints.

Once the organization settles on the desired development process, work with engineering management to set up a kick-off meeting to explain the process to the rest of the organization and prepare it for implementation. It is critical that everyone clearly understands and appreciates his or her role in the process, expected milestones, and benchmarks. Decide who will be the champion of the process to keep things rolling and who will resolve conflicts or issues.

The Product Manager does not participate in the actual development process—that's the job of engineering. The PM rather monitors progress of the development process as one of the overall product development functions. To maintain consensus on targets and goals, progress should be documented and readily available to all participants across the company. An Intranet or other online repository is an ideal place to house progress and other critical documents that are part of the development cycle. Keep in mind, however, that too much documentation can bog down development. Because most people do not like creating or reading paperwork, select only that which is critical to the process. Large companies with large and scattered development staffs often build complicated, document-intensive project management systems that attempt to define every single aspect of the development process. For smaller companies, on the other hand, verbose progress reporting is to be avoided. It can be a distraction and an unnecessary drain on resources.

To avoid over-documentation of progress, build a step right into the development process itself that makes sure the team revisits the process during and after each cycle. Hold formal debriefings that result in updating the process document as need be. This will allow the team to evaluate the process and refine it as time goes by. Don't expect the development process to be perfect out of the gate. Processes of any kind must adapt as the needs of the organization change. A good process adapts as things change and as the organization learns more about itself and its capabilities.

An Example Development Process: Base Level Integration Planning (BLIP)

A specific process called Base Level Integration Planning (BLIP) serves as an excellent template to get small and medium software companies started. It provides enough structure without getting in the way of creativity or exceeding resource limitations. The idea is somewhat revolutionary in that the entire process is based on time, rather than features. Many companies use a development process that begins with the Product Manager submitting a long list of requirements to engineering. Engineering then returns an estimate of time it will take them to develop all of the features. That amount of time subsequently defines the development cycle.

A major problem with this approach is that it has many points of failure that can cause it to be highly unreliable and unnecessarily time-consuming. For example, a cycle that is planned to be 6 months to complete a list of 10 new features can easily slip when one feature takes longer than expected or a key resource is not available. Unless the release has been carefully engineered to compensate for interdependencies of the features or the market/customers are flexible enough to accept changes in delivery, it is hard to stop a feature-based cycle and regroup in the middle. Further, the goal has been set to deliver the list of features that are used to measure personal and professional success. The list becomes the set of marching orders for the entire organization and therefore the failure of any one feature is then not viewed as an option. Time is, in fact, not the highest priority attribute with this approach, but rather the feature list is.

For a small company trying to be first to market and keep a competitive edge, time to market is everything. In addition, by delivering the product consistently on time and with quality, a company can build a reputation for reliability and effectiveness. Using a formal, yet adaptable, process should help achieve these goals.

The BLIP process is an example of a time-based development cycle. It starts with a schedule for each development cycle or Base Level (BL), and then builds a practical set of features and development work into the schedule, rather than the other way around. In software engineering, this approach is called "time boxing." By using the BLIP process, a company can maintain fleet-footedness and flexibility while ensuring functionality to keep ahead of the market. The BLIP process is flexible enough to allow the development team to focus on one of the development attributes (quality, functionality or time) as much or as little as desired for each release cycle.

The BLIP cycles overlap. They are designed to keep the ball

moving at all times and to optimize development and quality assurance resources. By working the way the process works, companies can deliver essential functionality while simultaneously refining requirements as they change. When new features are required, they are a "BLIP away" from delivery. Unlike feature-based processes, the BLIP lets the organization break things into manageable small parts so that it doesn't get stuck with a long release cycle that, in the end, doesn't work properly or misses the market opportunity.

From a management view, the BLIP process helps to avoid surprises. Because of its intense planning phase, it highlights, up front, the interdependencies that exist across multiple project teams. By having frequent, measurable and visible milestones, major slips in expected delivery dates can be avoided. When projects or resources are unavoidably misestimated, it is easier to make corrections during the cycle because the process allows the team to deal with these issues on a frequent basis.

From a quality perspective, the BLIP process operates on the assumption that "early discovery yields cheaper recovery." Performing system testing and integration on an iterative basis during the product development cycle offers a greater likelihood of discovering errors earlier, rather than later when they are harder to detect and correct. Frequent reviews and modifications to the process also allow the organization to build a self-optimizing environment for product development, subsequently increasing the predictability and overall quality of the software product being delivered.

The BLIP process was created by adapting the concepts of the well-known Six Sigma process used in hardware manufacturing at many companies, most notably, Motorola. The BLIP process has been used at dozens of software companies where process is respected and delivery time is critical.

The process begins with a BLIP schedule. Typically, the schedule will span between 8-20 weeks (not including beta testing) but can be adjusted as needed for each organization, and for each individual product Base Level. Because the phases overlap, a 20-week schedule can mean that every 14 weeks, a new version of the software is ready for alpha testing (pre-customer testing, done by non-engineering personnel within the company).

A fundamental element of the BLIP is that not every Base Level (BL) will create a commercially available version—dubbed "Generally Available" (GA) or "First Revenue Shipment" (FRS) versions. For a start-up company, the first few BLs may be short, perhaps 10 weeks, to allow the product to get to market fast and maintain competitive advantage during critical market formation stages. More established companies might choose to extend the process timing, as they are better off not delivering too much software, too often. Some companies use a cycle of base levels that have different lengths (e.g. a long, development-heavy BL followed by a short quality-focused BL). As noted above, the length of the BL can change over time to reflect the company's needs, the maturity of the engineering organization, the market requirements, number of customers, and the product's life cycle itself.

Some important intangible ingredients must be present in order for the BLIP process to work effectively:

- A clear and swift decision-making process
- A single individual with authority to make binding decisions for any of the teams
- An atmosphere conducive to the free flow of information between and among the project teams. Source code and detailed design documents (when available) should be accessible to every project member. It is important to note that just because a design document is accessible to every member of the product team, it doesn't mean that it must be written with the intense care and level of explanation that would be appropriate for an external audience. Use the format and language that fits the specific organization's needs.
- An understanding of the interdependencies of each team upon one another. Decisions should be based upon what is good for the project as a whole, not based upon what is good for one team at the expense of another.

- A good software quality automation tool that supports defect tracking, testing, load balancing, customer enhancement requests, performance management, code management and configuration management

BLIP Definitions

The BLIP process operates in the context of a development organization where there are sets of small project teams cooperating to build a multi-component, complex software product. (A "project team" can in fact be a single individual.)

A *project* is the main unit of work defined in the BL plan. Projects to be started in a particular BL will be defined during the planning phase. At the start of BL, there will be new projects as well as ongoing projects that are carried over from previous BLs.

As the BLIP process is used to manage overall engineering resources during the time of a specific BL, the document may also include projects that are not considered actual deliverables in the product. Examples might be research for future requirements, internal projects, or resources needed to support other organizations in pre-sales or post-sales activities.

Each BL requires a number of roles to be filled by the engineering team (not the Product Manager). A role is defined by the activities, responsibilities and skills required by the individual as part of the cycle.

BLIP Roles include:

- A *BL Program Manager* is the person responsible for editing and driving the development of the Base Level Integration Plan and making operational decisions on development issues that cross team boundaries. This person should be, or report to, a common manager of the teams. In smaller companies, the Program Manager may in fact be the Engineering Manager or VP.
- A *BL Project Leader* describes a person that is responsible for a

particular project within the Base Level. The Project Leader for new projects will be identified during BL planning. The Project Leader will provide the written BL plan for his or her project. Project Leaders can and should change from one BL to another to allow for Engineers to gain exposure to new parts of the product and to create a more knowledgeable development team.

- A *BL Team Leader* describes a person that is responsible for all activity within a narrowly focused area. This area may be a technological area of the product such as 3rd party integration, or it may be a service-focused area such as customer support. Team Leaders should also be rotated from one BL to another unless they are working on projects that require more than a single BL.

- An *Individual Contributor* is assigned to one or more project teams. The individual contributor will receive work assignments during each base level from a Project Leader.

Another important aspect of the BLIP process is *System Integration*. System Integration is the name of both a process and a specific team. The System Integration team may have a variety of activities. Among those is the responsibility for performing automated test systems utilized by project teams. The formal members of the team are responsible for development and maintenance of the system integration infrastructure. At times various members of other teams will do system integration work. Almost every individual should participate in system integration at one time or another.

Other important definitions that are used during a BL are:

- **BLn**. Every Base Level is named with a number (e.g., BL1, BL2, and so on). In describing generic Base Levels, the notation BLn will be used.

Base Level Integration Planning (BLIP)
Core Engineering Activities

Planning	*Implementation*	*Integration*	
△	△	△	△
BLn	**BLn**	**BLn**	**BLn**
Start	Planned	Built	Verified

- **BLn Planning.** This is the planning phase of the Base Level. During this phase the Program Manager, Team Leaders and Project Leaders define the work that needs to be accomplished during that Base Level.
- **BLn Planned.** This denotes the milestone that the BLn planning phase for Base Level "n" has been completed.
- **BLn Implementation.** This represents the implementation phase for the Base Level. During this phase the project leaders, developers, integration team and individual contributors are working toward delivering the work committed to during the planning phase.
- **BLn Built.** This represents the milestone of completing the BLn implementation phase for Base Level "n."
- **BLn Integration.** This represents the phase of the Base Level when all the project code deliverables are integrated and tested.
- **BLn Verified.** This represents the completion of Base Level "n." The achievement of this milestone does not necessarily imply a new release of the product. Software at this phase is ready to go to alpha testing and possible beta thereafter.

Here is how the BLIP process works: The complete BLIP is broken up into 6 phases: *Planning, Implementation, System Integration, Alpha Testing/Internal Handover, Beta Testing/First Customer Shipment (FCS), and General Availability/First Revenue Shipment (FRS).* These phases are carried out for each Base Level.

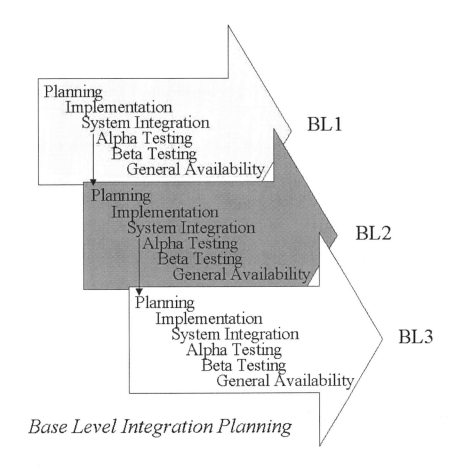

Base Level Integration Planning

1. Planning

Initial Planning Meeting

To kick off the phase, the Product Manager presents the engineering group with prioritized product requirements *(Chapter 3 on Product Requirements provides more information).* During the Planning phase, the Product Manager, BL Program Manager and BL Team Leaders will work together to ensure there is deep understanding of the requirements and they will scope out the time and resources required to accomplish each request. This may involve preliminary design of the feature to bound the scope and identify the implications from a product destabilization or testing point-of-view. Additional specifications may be necessary at this time. Other projects will also be identified that require engineering resources such as sales support, installation, customer care or internal technical infrastructure (e.g., system support, and back ups). Overall requirements will be broken down into projects with initial time and resource estimates.

Engineering and product management will then negotiate to decide the final list of projects to be done in that BL. Both Product Manager and the Engineering Manager should sign off on the list. The BL Program Manager and BL Team Leaders will then select the appropriate BL Project Leaders.

Plan Development

Project Leaders initiate detailed planning and prepare a written description of new or changed functionality that each of the projects will contribute to base level integration, including task resource allocation. Each team's contribution will contain detailed information regarding project activities and changes in functionality that could be visible to other teams.

Typically the written contribution for each team will be a few pages. This contribution should be in the form of a file that can easily be integrated into the overall planning document.

The Program Manager collates each of the Project Leaders' contributions and produces the draft of the Base Level Integration Plan. A date is set for the meeting to review the draft. The draft is distributed to each of the Team Leaders, Project Leaders and Project Members at least 3-5 working days prior to the meeting. This meeting is usually set for about 5-7 days prior to the expected *planned* date.

The Program Manager, Team Leaders and Project Leaders work together to identify and resolve any issues that are raised in the second draft of the plan. The ideal goal here is to enter the meeting with no outstanding issues.

Prepare for Plan Commitment

The Project Leaders should also confer with each of the individual contributors to ensure that the team can commit to the work listed in the draft. A Project Leader is usually unable to commit for his or her team unless they have developed a detailed schedule with each of the members of the team.

It is important to remember for each project team to schedule time to contribute to the System Integration process. This will typically range from a half a person to more than half of the team, depending upon the stage of the project.

Final Planning Meeting

The BL Program Manager should moderate this meeting. One of the primary objectives of this meeting is to resolve any outstanding issues in the Base Level Integration Plan. Any outstanding issues not already resolved by this point are automatically escalated to the Program Manager for resolution. Possible additional topics for discussion at this meeting include:

- A report on the overall status of the development effort against the expected delivery date.
- Proposals or discussion of possible process improvements.
- Review of plans for future architecture work.
- Any major risks to the planned product delivery date or to the expected functionality of the product delivered.

Prepare and Distribute Final BLIP Document Draft

The BL Program Manager is responsible for rapidly updating and distributing the final draft of the Base Level Plan. At this point, every team and project leader probably has the pertinent parts of the plan memorized!

At the "BL Planned" milestone, Engineering will have a solid list of specific projects, people and estimates on what will be built during the cycle. The idea is to remove all guesswork as to what and how these things will be built during the Implementation phase. While there are books upon books on how to estimate software projects, this activity, for the most part, still remains an art.

As the BLIP process is used, be sure to focus on previous requirements phases and how well the organization all did with their estimations. Refining the organization's abilities to estimate development time is as valuable as refining sales forecasting skills. It is quite natural that engineers will "pad" their estimates so that they are able to meet their commitments. If the organization allows this, the development team will not be operating at peak efficiency. Engineers should have the goal that some of their estimates are below actual delivery time and some are above, but they *average* out to be as accurate as possible. Make sure that overestimating is not rewarded or encouraged. Using the time to carefully plan out a release is what allows the BLIP process to be highly reliable and predictable. Typically, the Requirements Phase is 2-4 weeks long, but allow enough time to do a thorough job in this planning phase. The end result will be the development plan for that specific BLIP *(See sample BLIP plan in Appendix A)*.

The BL Plan is formally signed at the *planned* milestone.

2. Implementation

This is the part of the cycle where actual software development is accomplished. The code is written and unit-tested during this heads-down phase in which engineers are actually creating the software. It is also an ideal time for Product Managers to begin working on collateral and other communications materials, searching for beta sites, and setting up internal alpha testers.

The implementation phase for a given base level depends on every company's defined cycle. Development tasks don't naturally fit into any particular duration, but there is virtue in having a uniform, predictable number to facilitate long-term planning. The analogy here is one of a train (BLn) that leaves the station regularly on a predictable schedule. The baggage (requirements or product features) that makes it onto the train continues through implementation and system integration. All requirements that miss the scheduled train wait for the next train (BLn+1).

Allowing the train to leave without all the planned functionality requires great discipline but is the key to developing a reliable, quality process. What makes this palatable is that another train is on its way in a matter of a few weeks. Though it takes a little while for organizations to get used to this way of thinking and acting, the benefits found from maintaining a predictable and reliable release cycle outweigh the temptation to extend a release date to include a planned feature. Even when large, perhaps paid for, features are missed, the BLIP cycle only works if the trains leave on time. Once a train is held back, the entire process is in jeopardy and creates a negative domino effect on reliability of the process. Remember that the BLIP process is designed to manage time as the primary element. If the organization is not committed to this basic premise, the BLIP process will not be effective. Perhaps more psychological than anything else, the BLIP process helps organizations be very conscious of their own development capabilities in a space of time rather than in their overall ability to complete a task. It values strong forecasting and careful planning, thus resulting in a more reliable and consistent development process.

Formal Implementation Checkpoint

Each week, each Project Leader must report to the Program Manager on his or her team's preparedness for the *built* milestone. Tasks should be described in measurable terms in order to eliminate ambiguity about achieving objectives. It is useful to measure the time remaining to complete items rather than the percentage complete. When using percentages, it is common that engineers will report that 90% of the overall project is complete but in truth the last 10% of the functionality may take 90% of the time to complete, making percentages meaningless.

As noted previously, despite good planning, it is possible that some projects will not be completed on time. Personnel changes, unexpected equipment problems, poor development estimation and acts of God can cause some of the projects not to be completed as expected. In these hopefully rare cases, the Program Manager and the Product Manager will need to discuss the impact of dropping specific functionality or objectives to allow the *built* date to be met. This is the preferred course of action to take unless the team or functionality in question is known or suspected to be on the critical path for the project as a whole. As discussed above, changing the *built* date is a cardinal "no-no." Over time, the organization will be able to anticipate unexpected issues to account for them in the BL plan.

Within a given project, the Project Leader is responsible for the management and migration of individual source files from one internally consistent version of a facility to another. Use of modern source control and configuration management system tools across each of the teams is important to manage a complex project. Source control tools can also assist a team in managing code check-in/out, security, labeling, branching, backup, the ability to rebuild labeled releases and other critical activities that must be organized across the development team.

Each Project Leader is responsible for determining whether the facilities are ready at *built* level. They are also responsible for communicating that they have achieved the BLn *built* level for the specific version or facility. There are two important criteria behind this declaration:

- All functionality is complete
- The facility has been unit tested, meaning that all the major code paths have been executed successfully at least once. In order to accomplish unit testing in a timely and cost-effective manner, it may be necessary to create component-level tests or a component-level test harness. A component-level test harness is used to exercise a facility without requiring the remaining parts of the system to be present.

Once all the projects are declared *built*, system implementation is considered complete. By the end of the implementation phase, the Product Manager needs to prepare the requirements document for the next BL cycle. As implementation is completed, Engineering goes back into the Planning phase again for the next BL.

3. System Integration

At this point, control of the BL passes to the System Integration team that is responsible for administering the build process and doing an initial viability test of the product. A viability test establishes that the product works well enough that it is ready to test. When this process is mature, the expectation is that this step can be automated. The System Integration phase is a validation that the product as a whole works properly with the newly integrated features. System Integration should take at least 2 weeks and no longer than 3. Keep in mind that this is not testing the functionality of the code itself, but rather testing the integration of the various parts. During development, developers will be unit testing each part and once brought together, both system and functional testing can commence.

System Testing Begins

The *built* version of the product must undergo automated regression testing and is used for development and maintenance of system-level tasks. Each of the development teams is responsible for the development of some segment of proactive system testing activity utilizing the built version of the product. The System Integration (SI) group should be involved in defining and building unit test scripts during implementation. This approach allows the SI team to become familiar with the code very early in the process and then adequately prepare themselves for system integration testing when the final *built* code is made available.

The System Integration team is responsible for administering the build system, the automated regression test system and the internal problem reporting system. System testing activities that encounter problems are triaged by a member of the System Integration team. Problem reports are assigned to a particular team based on the facility that likely caused the problem.

Each Project Leader is responsible for designating a team contact that will be responsible for working that problem or directly passing it on to another member of the team. The policy for how the problem is managed within the team is at the discretion of the Project Leader. This is referred to as passive System Integration activity. The general project policy is that passive System Integration activities are a higher priority than new development tasks but must be accounted for as new BLs are planned.

Review of the Test Reports

During the period of time between *built* and verified, once each week (or more often if needed), the System Integration Team Leader or the Program Manager should hold a brief meeting. This meeting reviews the status of all outstanding problems in the internal problem reporting system. A member from each team attends and verbally reports on the status of any outstanding problems that are assigned to that team. It is important that all identified problems are prioritized so that the development team can handle them efficiently.

Base Level Verified

The Program Manager reviews information provided by the System Integration team and Project Leaders, and declares the Base Level version *verified* when the quality objectives have been satisfied.

The *verified* version of the product is made available for possible distribution. It can undergo further testing, be used in demos, or shipped to customers.

Knowledge Transfer

After the version is *verified*, the System Integration team working with the Product Manager will provide technical knowledge transfer to various groups within the company. New features, new functionality, operational differences, and installation and configuration changes from previous versions will be highlighted. Knowledge transfer will be targeted to a number of departments including: Product Management, Training, Solutions Engineering and Customer Support, to ensure successful product delivery.

Conduct Post-Mortem

The overall idea of Base Level Integration Planning is to produce a high quality software product on a predictable schedule. However, as humans, mistakes will be made. A post-mortem of the base level should be conducted after every cycle. The Program Manager will drive this process. The Base Level template should be updated to reflect the lessons learned during the base level cycle. The new version then gets used for the next BLIP plan and the cycle continues.

As the system integration phase comes to an end, the Product Manager needs to have his or her beta sites lined up and paper work just about filed. Chapter 5 provides more information on Beta Testing.

4. Alpha Testing and Internal Handover

A short and intensive internal testing period really helps iron out any issues before they land at a customer site. Identify a handful of qualified internal individuals, including the Product Manager, to exercise the product and to exercise the new features in as much of a real-world way as possible. If possible, use real sample data and try to emulate an actual customer. Having replicated customer environments and previous "uses" of the product in place is an excellent way to augment "backwards compatibility" testing as well as accuracy (the ability of the product to reproduce the same results). Doing this for key customers also helps ensure that major problems will be detected before the product is in use.

Provide written feedback to the engineers on issues that come up. Ideally, these issues are logged using the same automated bug tracking system that was used by the other constituents during the development process. To allow internal (non-engineering) people to do the testing, engineering may need to provide some form of training and user documentation. If the company has a consulting group that works directly with customers, they are ideal to participate in alpha testing. Training can be informal but should allow for hands-on experiences. Have a single engineering person ("The Testing or Quality Assurance (QA) Manager") manage this phase so users know where to go for support and that there is a single person to funnel issues to. Because alpha testing is not part of one's routine job, the Testing Manager will have to carefully monitor progress and ensure that testing is getting done correctly. The Testing Manager might want to have each tester submit a test plan of what they plan to do and the Testing Manager may need to direct testing plans somewhat to help ensure complete coverage. This period can be short if all are committed to it. One to two weeks should be more than sufficient for this phase.

When detected, bugs should be reported in the bug tracking system and engineering should be reviewing and addressing them on a priority basis. Engineering may need to have daily meetings to review outstanding issues, assign them appropriately and assess the rate at which new things are coming in and the organization's ability to fix them. Again as a reminder, do not forget to plan for this engineering time within the new BL that is just starting at this point. A fair amount of resources will be consumed to fix bugs before new functionality can be designed and implemented.

5. Beta Testing and First Customer Shipment (FCS)

Although beta testing is not truly an engineering process, it is an essential part of the development cycle, so it is included here *(see also Chapter 5 for more information on beta testing)*. The Product Manager will need support from engineering when bugs are identified. However, at this point in the cycle, most of engineering is already working on the next BLIP and should be heavily into implementation. Some companies refer to beta testing as First Customer Shipment (FCS) indicating that the product is now ready to be received by a customer, though not for revenue recognition purposes.

Note that larger software companies sometimes use external testers within Alpha testing and therefore declare FCS at that time. Because of the limited resources in smaller companies, it is recommended that the PM runs an internal Alpha and controlled beta to ensure a manageable process.

The Product Manager will be either running the beta testing program or at least intimately involved with it. Beta testing should involve all the people and systems that will be part of the final offering. The order processing system should also be tested during this time as well as the training and customer support systems to ensure the kinks are worked out of the entire offering.

Once the beta sites are lined up and test plans in place, software must now be must delivered to these testers. The company may need to install the software remotely or on-site or a CD or FTP site can be used to distribute the beta software to the testers to install themselves. If possible, use the same installation procedure that the final product will offer. Installation is a key part of the product experience and should be tested thoroughly. If the software is to be used in a hosted environment, a system needs to be set up and available for the users. The users should provide feedback on issues arising from the initial set up and logon.

A well-run beta test will provide ongoing feedback into the company and allow the software to be fixed as necessary. Continue using the same bug tracking system used throughout the development process to capture any new issues raised during beta testing. Engineering resources should remain assigned to the tasks of supporting the beta tests and correcting problems found during the process.

Beta testing will provide valuable input into marketing, revealing how users actually use and perceive the value of the new features. It will also provide ideas for future releases. Beta testing should last 30 – 90 days and concludes with the Product Delivery Team *(see Chapters 4 & 5)* making the final determination if the product is ready for revenue release. For the sake of the marketing team who will want to use beta sites as references in the press and other places, try to allow ample time to complete agreed upon activities and address any issues responsively so that these advocates are satisfied in the end.

6. General Availability Release and First Revenue Ship (FRS)

With the software successfully tested in the field, now celebrate the successful completion of the release and announce its availability to the world. Some companies call this First Revenue Ship (FRS) or General Availability. Some companies use an interim release that is more controlled to allow only certain customers access to the software. In either scenario, the product is now ready to be ordered through the standard mechanisms and the accounting group can invoice and subsequently recognize revenue for shipments.

Don't forget to celebrate. Congratulate the entire engineering team on the successful completion of a finished a Base Level Cycle! Send internal announcements, copy and escrow the final code, launch the product into the market, but most of all, enjoy the accomplishment of the most critical part of the process for delivering on time, quality software!

Chapter 3:
Managing Product Requirements

Gathering product requirements is both a science and an art form. Product requirements can come from many sources including customers, prospects, competitive analysis, and internally from within the organization. Product Managers may use a combination of formal and informal means to solicit the input. The Product Management challenge is to decide which requirements should be considered and why.

Art meets science here as PMs may have many quantitative and qualitative reasons why a requirement is important. Perhaps the new feature will directly meet a customer or prospect need and generate a new source of revenue. Or perhaps the requirement will enable the company to be more competitive and bring longer-term returns. Some requirements may be important because they represent architectural needs for the long-term development of the product (e.g. rewriting the code in a more flexible and cost effective development language) but might not make any noticeable difference to a customer. Other requirements may simply fix aspects of the product that don't work correctly or need more testing. PMs can create requirements that specify necessary research to examine future areas of potential development. Essentially think of a product requirement as anything that the Product Manager wants or needs the engineering group to spend time on during a development cycle. The requirements document winds up being a prioritized "wish list" of all the things that could be done.

Once the list is established, the next step is to flesh out those top priorities and be as specific as possible so that engineering is not second guessing what they "think" the PM wants. Depending on the development process that the company uses, the PM may need to reevaluate the list once engineering has determined the time, resources and possible technical impact involved in delivering each requirement. If the Base Level Integration Process is going to be used, each BL starts with a Requirements Phase that includes the gathering, prioritizing, justification and agreement of requirements before they are finalized and handed over to engineering for design and development.

Here are nine practical steps to carry out the seemingly daunting task of generating product requirements.

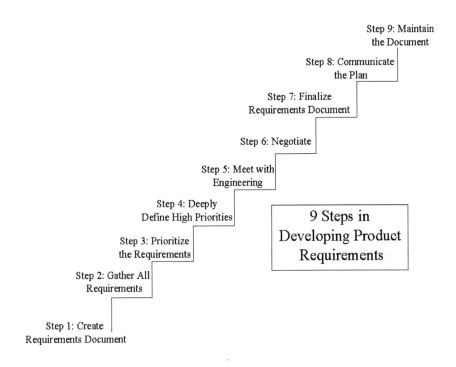

Step 1: Create the requirements document.

First establish an organized document, database or other repository to gather and manage the requirements. There are formal requirements tracking software tools on the market that can help. These systems help collect input, organize it, and maintain the source and other information for future use. Some systems can automatically generate a requirements document. Some systems even provide ongoing communication about development progress back to the sources of the requirements (which may or may not be desirable). The cost of these systems varies depending on vendor, version of the tool selected, and implementation used (hosted versus internally served). There are also open source bug tracking tools, some of which will allow limited customization to also use them as requirements tracking tools.

Alternatively, (or perhaps as a starting point), PMs can create a custom database or spreadsheet. Whatever tool is used, be sure to capture the information noted below and cross reference the requirements with the development process so that each requirement can be referred to easily. Essentially, the PM needs a place where (s)he can capture and organize and track requirements on an ongoing basis. The system should include at least the following attributes (columns):

- *Requirement Number* – Uniquely identify requirements for future reference. Reference numbers can be as simple as an incrementing item count. Consider creating categories so the requirements are easier to find and help maximize efficiency during the development process. If there are major changes being made in one area of the code, it's easy to knock off a bunch of other requirements in the same category. Categorizing requirements in this way makes it easy to find other related requests. It's good to look at related requests because many captured enhancements ask for similar "solutions" and it is important to make sure all captured "use cases" are considered to make sure the final solution handles all of the different requests. Be sure that the overall identification scheme helps support the categories and sub-categories. If the bug tracking system is used to record the items, it will most likely provide an automated numbering scheme. Be sure to tie the appropriate bug numbers in the tracking system to those noted in the requirements document.
- *Date Entered* – Note the date in which the requirement was entered into the document or system. If a requirement is collected from more than one source, be sure to note both sources and both dates.
- *Functional Description* – This should be a brief description of the requirements. Create and refer to a more detailed document to explain complex requirements more precisely. It can be helpful to have a one-line summary or title for each requirement to quickly identify or reference the specific entry.

- *Priority* – A priority code helps determine a sense of importance of the requirement. Indicate which requirements are urgent and need to be addressed right away versus other requirements that would be "nice to have" in the product, or ideas for future enhancements. Use a simple scheme (e.g. ranking them 1 – 5 or high/medium/low priority). When handling many customer requests, it may help to have 2 priority fields - one for the ranking that the organization assigns to the requirement, and the other one to indicate the priority that the customer or other source assigned.

- *Source* – Indicate from where or from whom the requirement originated. Be as specific as possible in naming not only that the requirement came from a customer or partner but which one. This will enable the organization to go back to the appropriate source if additional information is needed later and once implemented, that source can be notified that the feature is available. Capture the software release on which the request was made (e.g. Version 5.1.2).

- *Status* – As the requirements document is used throughout the development process moving from one version of the product to the next, keep notes on each requirement as it is added to a version. Note if the requirement is in development or still remains a requirement for future consideration. This will help anyone refer back to older versions to see what was added at that time.

- *Estimated Revenue Opportunity/Justification* – Here is where the PM provides quantitative and qualitative explanations of why the requirement is important. If the PM can quote a revenue amount, that is ideal. At a minimum, state why the requirement is needed and what will happen if it isn't added to the product.

- *Estimated Development Hours* – As the PM goes through the planning process with engineering, (s)he will get estimates for the various high priority requirements. Add this to the spreadsheet and if that requirement does not make the current development cycle, it will be available for future planning.

- *Return on Investment (ROI)* – This simplistic form of ROI calculation is the estimated revenue minus the estimated cost (cost = development hours times a fully loaded hourly rate).

The output of the database or spreadsheet becomes the Requirements Document *(See sample requirements document in Appendix B)*. It is the heart and soul of the process by which PMs gather, track and manage the product development lifecycle. In fact, PMs can use it perpetually to track and review development as it occurs from cycle to cycle. In this way, the PM will not lose ideas and can adjust priorities as needed over time. The Requirements Document can also serve as an archived list for features as they are added to the product. This will come in handy when the PM needs to recall, "which features were added when". Product Managers find themselves referring to the Requirements Document often for financial auditing, answering RFPs (Request for Proposals) and many other activities that require them to remember when specific items were added to the product.

Step 2: Gather all requirements.

Sources for Product Requirements

Sales

Engineering & Technical Support

Customers

Partners

Product Manager

Competitive Analysis

Other Employees

Prospects

Industry Analysts & Consultants

Product Managers get requirements from many sources on an ongoing basis. For example, every time a PM presents the product, most likely someone will ask if the product can do "x." If the PM's answer is "no," this should be noted in the requirements list. Though it may not seem important at that moment, it helps to have the requirement for future reference. When someone else asks a second time, it will be good to know that it was requested before.

When someone has an idea for a new feature, it is a good practice to ask "why?" What specifically are they trying to accomplish? Ask them if there are alternative ways to address the issue they are raising, perhaps by using existing product capabilities. Moreover, try to assess the value of each feature and if it really makes a difference in someone's use or purchase decision. Be sure to ask: "What is the real benefit of the new feature? What is the impact of *not* putting it in the product? How much are customers willing to pay for the feature?" The PM should consider how the new feature will change the product and if that is in line with the company's strategic plans. Despite the customer's suggestion appearing to be good, it may require a major change in the product or product direction that is not so good after all. All requirements should be gathered and weighed as objectively as possible. The job of the Product Manager is to determine which requirements are priorities and which are not.

The technical support group is a vital and ongoing source of requirements. Whether they have a formal way to capture issues or customer ideas, or if a more formal meeting is called with them regularly, be sure to listen very closely. As a primary customer interface, the support team can provide first-hand knowledge about what works in the product and what doesn't. They will also have ideas on ways to fix or optimize the product, including its documentation. PMs can gain tremendous insight into the product through technical support teams — build a strong alliance with them.

The engineering group will undoubtedly be a gold mine of requirements information. As with the support team, it is a good idea to meet frequently with the engineers. Let them freely share their ideas. While they may not present a customer's perspective as well as some others in the organization, engineers have a very unique view of the product that they are building. They are always looking for ways to make it work better or extend its capabilities.

If possible, it is great to get engineers listening directly to customer feedback. In small companies, engineers sometimes participate in support calls or on-site visits. The more the engineers are plugged into the users, the more they will understand how the product is perceived, how it is actually used, and the issues around using it effectively. If focus groups are used, be sure to involve engineers. Bridging the gap between the engineers who know the technology in depth and the people who use it, can really help a PM to make the product "customer-focused."

The other critical internal group to stay close to is sales. Salespeople will be loaded with ideas on how to improve the product. A common statement from salespeople is "they can sell a bundle if the product only had a particular feature or two". Don't be swayed by this habit of selling the future. Despite such pining, the sales group can indeed provide invaluable competitive information. If the sales people do win/loss reports, analyze those closely. Understand, however, that the reports will naturally have some biases in them because they are written from the sales perspective and not the prospects'. Salespeople can provide very valuable, although often subjective, inputs—esthetic changes or other small enhancements to help demonstrate value to customers.

Be wary of salespeople promising potential revenue unless they can quote a customer who said they would purchase the product or add-on if a specific feature is added. Don't get caught in the vicious cycle of "our next release will be the winner." Salespeople will always want more, for the lack of functionality is a convenient excuse for why they aren't selling more of the product. To them, a lack of sales is always a direct result of a product weakness, and not due to a lack of sales talent! Take the input seriously though, and make sure when a need is identified, find out where it is coming from and why.

Other people in the organization will come forward with ideas. Everyone from the company President to the accountants to the lawyers will have requirements to contribute such as essential trademark information, in-code product disclosures and license information. A great way to kick-off a requirements phase is by issuing an internal memo or email soliciting product ideas throughout the organization. Many great ideas will also come from casual conversations and brainstorming meetings. Figure out who really knows the product or market and keep in touch with them regularly. Create a list of people who can contribute to the requirements and make sure their input is solicited during the requirements phase.

Externally, there are many places to go for requirements. One essential tool needed for opening dialogues about future plans with external sources is a non-disclosure agreement (NDA). *(An NDA template is provided in Appendix C.)* The NDA legally binds third parties to hold information in confidence and not use it in a way that represents a competitive threat to the company. If a general NDA is already in place that covers proprietary information shared with that person or company, it may not be necessary to have them sign a specific NDA for requirements planning. Some companies include NDA language in their sales contracts between customers and partners. NDA language is even present in most employment contracts. NDAs are a typical part of the software business so be sure there is one in place before product plans are discussed with external parties.

Business partners such as VARs (value added resellers) and OEMs (original equipment manufacturers) will have great ideas on how to improve the product. Much like the internal sales force, business partners are also motivated to see new features that will help them sell more product. Their perspective is very different from other audiences and depending on their relationship with the company, the PM may decide to lean heavily on the partners' say so. No doubt that more weight is given to partners who are dependent on the software product such as OEMs rather than casual marketing partners. When the business partners have their own skin in the game and are dependent the product for their own success, they tend to be much more rational on the product's features and functions.

Definitely look at how the partner ties the product and specific feature requests to its own business plans. Like the other inputs from other audiences, ask for business justification on each requirement to be sure that the "why" and cost benefit for each feature or function is clearly understood and appreciated.

Depending on the company and product, customers may be constantly demanding new bells and whistles. Some customers pay an annual maintenance fee to continue using the product and to automatically qualify for new releases. Because customers can demand new features that are not revenue producing, PMs will have to judge the importance of the requests. As such, new requirements from existing customers can be hard to justify since the new features may not generate additional revenue directly. Regardless of the revenue implication, listen carefully to the customer's input and ask the question, "If the new feature is not added, will it cause any customers to discontinue using the product?"

Having used the product extensively, customers may see ways to improve the product to make it more competitive or more valuable. Note their ideas in the requirements document and try to quantify the return on additional investment by bouncing the ideas off other customers. While it may not generate more direct revenues from existing customers, does this requirement help sell upgrade versions or perhaps new components to the existing product base? The most productive way to gain happy customers is to make sure they know they are being listened to. Involving them in the requirements process is one way to let them know that their input is important.

In smaller and start-up companies, reference or showcase accounts are critical to launching major sales initiatives. Requirements coming from these accounts may carry more weight than other sources because they *must* be happy customers if they are to be used as reference or showcase examples. Be extremely careful with what is promised. Only that which can actually be delivered counts with this special class of customers. If they have been designated showcases, they will inevitably know they have some power with the company. Don't let that power be abused in a way that directs the product to their needs only. Do keep in mind, however, that if there is a disciplined and explainable process, these customers will respect it and be honored to participate in it as long as they know their ideas are being heard and considered appropriately.

Focus groups can be used to solicit customer input. In-person meetings and formal focus groups are certainly desirable, but they may be costly or prohibited by time constraints. Webcasting offers a great way to quickly show and discuss new ideas and have small groups interact with each other, bouncing feedback between the company and their customers. Webcasts are great for less in-depth discussions where a lot of time is not needed to address a particular topic or issue. Webcasting systems provide tools for interaction such as live software demonstration and whiteboard tools. They can be effective but won't have the benefit of seeing an audience's body language. As a result, webcasting isn't recommended for products with a lot of interactive features or user interface issues where the PM wants to see firsthand how easy or attractive something is to the user.

Most customers feel they are "entitled" to a more personal touch that that provided by webcasting. Some will feel more comfortable with the medium than others, making it a challenge to get the whole group involved. Most people can't sit in front of a computer for long periods of time talking to a screen and listening to a faceless voice. Balance the use of high-tech webcasting or teleconferencing with high-touch forms of research. Webcasting works particularly well with technology partners, as they tend to be more comfortable with the medium and virtual meetings.

Blogs and podcasts are being used more and more to solicit and collect customer feedback. A podcast is essentially a pre-recorded audio or video (vodcast or vidcast) file that can be viewed online. Depending on how is it is set up, the file can be downloaded and listened to or viewed on an appropriate device such as a computer or iPod. This allows a user to take the file and experience the content anytime – perhaps while exercising, traveling, and so on. Some podcast sites allow the user to listen to or view the podcast from the server where it is hosted. This alternative method may be instead of or in addition to allowing a user to download the podcast on to his or her own device of choice. Typically, podcasts are in MP3 format for audio, and vodcasts in MPEG format. Consider using a podcast to record audio or video information about the product. A product demonstration, training, or presentation can be recorded and distributed to appropriate audiences.

Another useful tool for solicitng requirements can be a blog. Per the definition in Wikipedia, "A blog is a website where entries are made in journal style and displayed in a reverse chronological order. Blogs often provide commentary or news on a particular subject, such as food, politics, or local news. Some function as more personal online diaries. A typical blog combines text, images, and links to other blogs, web pages, and other media related to its topic. Most blogs are primarily textual although some focus on photographs (photoblog), videos (vlog), or audio (podcasting), and are part of a wider network of social media."

Use a Blog to encourage multi-directional conversation about the product. Consider setting up an RSS link to a blog or other posting areas that will automatically inform the involved members when new content (documents, posts, and so on) are available. The goal is to build a community for the specific purposes of collecting product requirements.

A wiki can also be used to provide a forum for all product stakeholders to contribute their ideas freely. Again according to the best known wiki, Wikipedia, "A wiki is a type of website that allows the visitors themselves to easily add, remove and otherwise edit and change some available content, sometimes without the need for registration. This ease of interaction and operation makes a wiki an effective tool for collaborative authoring." All of these Web 2.0 technologies are relatively inexpensive and effective. As a software provider, it is important to use these relatively new methods to reflect the company's overall innovation and willingness to use new technology.

Other great product management tools include online surveys. These can be easily created and administered quickly and cheaply using one of the many online survey providers on the web. Online surveys allow a PM to ask customers (and others) their opinions to identify trends or review open ended comments. These survey engines are not only easy to use, they are inexpensive. Surveys can be embedded into newsletters, pointed to from blogs and wikis, or included in other communications. The survey results are automatically tabulated and viewed online. Most products offer the ability to download result data and use it with a favorite graphing package.

However it is done, talk with and listen to customers often. Design a process to reach out and touch customers and prospects regularly. Continuous customer contact is the only way to truly validate that the product is on target.

Prospective buyers are also great bearers of requirements information. They see the product very differently than anyone else. If they are new to the type of product or technology, they may not be able to comment on each feature or lack of features. They can, however, give invaluable feedback such as the ease-of-use or impression that the product leaves on a fresh set of eyes. Prospects may come to a discussion with preconceived ideas about how such a product should work. From this viewpoint, they may share some truly innovative ideas and surprises. If they have been evaluating other similar or competitive products, they can help compare and contrast products. Competitors may not seem to have a beautiful "baby" but market perception is everything. Interacting with prospects at trade shows, seminars, via telemarketing campaigns, Blogs, message boards, and so on, can also bring input into the cycle that helps show what is expected in the market and help position and prioritize product capabilities. Check out the competitors' blogs or other third party portals that gather product information. Anything that can be found is helpful.

In addition to talking directly with prospects, review Requests for Proposals/Information (RFPs) /(RFIs). These are essentially one prospect's own specific requirements for the product. Keep in mind, however, that RFPs may be a ruse. RFPs are sometimes used to justify the selection of an already chosen vendor. This kind of RFP is considered "wired" as the requirements are biased toward those features offered by the already chosen vendor. Sometimes RFPs are used by companies only to test a company's future commitment to them as future customers. Sometimes RFPs are used to see if an "ideal" set of features exists or is planned by vendors. Because responding to RFPs can take enormous amounts of time and resources from a company, be sure that there is a fair opportunity to compete for the business before expending resources. In addition, make sure that the working and structure of the RFP allows for all participants to accurately represent the capabilities of their offering. If not, get back to the prospective buyer and address any concerns about the RFP.

Competitive information is a significant source of requirements information and assists in virtually everything done by a Product Manager. Thorough competitive analysis is vital to success and what can be uncovered is comparable to Thomas Edison's notion that "ideas are in the air." Both content and context ideas are sure to surface, and ideas in the air can be "borrowed". Just be careful not to infringe on any patents, copyrights, or trademarks.

Being able to understand competitors and the target market requires casting a wide net, including web information, analyst reports, investors, consultants, and trade publications. Be creative and ultimately try to find a way to get hands-on experience with competing products. It may even be worth the time and cost to purchase the competitive products because seeing is believing. Not only will new features be exposed, it is incredibly helpful to see how someone else approached similar software challenges and how they implemented their own solutions. Another reminder, borrow carefully.

Regardless of the sources for requirements information, always ask "why" as well as "what." Don't just judge the importance of the requirements information from a development perspective, but rather a customer and revenue perspective. Try to get the source to explain how specific features work and how the feature changes the way the product is used. *How and why a product is used is more important than what the product does.* Software products can fail, despite being more robust than competitive products. They may fail due to a lack of esthetics, simple features, ease of use, help facilities, or documentation. Recall the Sony Betamax video machines, the Digital Rainbow PC, OS2, object-relational databases and many other state-of-the-art products that came and went. Their Product Managers forgot that successful technology is not necessarily more advanced, but rather, it's better matched to *perceived* market needs and preferences.

Prototypes and proof-of-concept projects can be a tremendous resource to flesh out product requirements that look great on paper but don't really fly when implemented. These activities serve as a source of discovery and analysis of product requirements prior to production-level software development. For more complex features, prototyping allows the work to be split into phases, gaining feedback at each phase. The philosophy is to avoid spending weeks, months or years before finding out that the requirement is wrong or has changed. During prototyping and proof-of-concept projects, constant feedback processes and metrics are critical. As with carpentry, it's far better to measure twice and cut once. Every $1 spent at this will save the equivalent of $5 to make corrections later in the product's lifecycle—that's the inherent ROI when requirements are done right.

Step 3: Prioritize the requirements.

Now that requirements specifications are gathered, the next step is to see what qualitative or quantitative benefits each will bring to the product. Because many variables are involved, a balanced scorecard approach can help. While the Chief Financial Officer (CFO) may want to see hard numbers for return on investment (ROI) factored into the development plan, the balanced scorecard goes beyond just specifying a dollar value for each project. It can help show what must be done to seize new business opportunities, what can be done to optimize business development, and what can be done to gain competitive advantage by delighting customers with usability features.

Robert S. Kaplan and David P. Norton, developers of the Balanced Scorecard method, write, "The balanced scorecard retains traditional financial measures. But financial measures tell the story of past events, an adequate story for industrial age companies for which investments in long-term capabilities and customer relationships were not critical for success. These financial measures are inadequate, however, for guiding and evaluating the journey that Information Age companies must make to create future value through investment in customers, suppliers, employees, processes, technology and innovation."

More than a financial measurement system, the Balanced Scorecard, is a strategic management system for achieving long-term goals. Kaplan and Norton show how to use measures in four categories—*financial performance, customer knowledge, internal business processes*, and *learning and growth*—to align individual, organizational and cross-company initiatives and to identify entirely new processes for meeting customer and shareholder objectives. The four perspectives provide a balance between short-term and long-term performance and include subjective as well as objective measures. Measures may include process cycle-time, transaction per employee ratios, cost per transaction, volume of transactions, percent of customers supported with digital customer care systems and time to fulfill service requests.

Some companies use the Kano methodology to help prioritize requirements. Developed in the 1980s, the Kano analysis allows PMs to prioritize requirements as a function of customer satisfaction. Kano defined four categories into which each feature or requirement can be classified: 1. Surprise and delight, 2. More is better, 3. Must be, and, 4. Better not be. Once categorized, the requirements are then graphed and looked at in terms of ROI.

However, a simpler, yet effective approach for smaller companies categorizes product requirements into three rankings: High, Medium and Low. "High" means the requirement needs to be incorporated in the very next cycle to generate revenue or support a strategic initiative. "Medium" means the requirement should be incorporated if resources are available beyond those needed for priority one. "Low" means "nice to have," but not critical to the next release cycle.

Requirements

High = Must have in this release/quantifiable revenue
Medium = Would be good to have/competitive feature/improved customer satisfaction
Low = Not required at this time/keep on the list for future consideration

Step 4: Define the "high" priorities.

With the top priorities identified, PMs now need to carefully consider how well the requirements are defined. A requirement such as "support for Oracle 10g Release 2" may be specific enough. However, it may need to be more specific to indicate whether the whole product or only parts should run in that environment. Consider issues such as whether the product must run with a particular native operating system support, if there are any differences between the development and runtime environments, and whether the software is expected to achieve specific performance metrics such as some number of transactions per second. Some requirements will require a lot more detail. A requirement such as "improve the user interface" or "provide an easier installation" warrant a few paragraphs or pictures on what exactly is desired. The more detail that can be provided, the fewer the surprises in the end. Never assume anyone, including (or perhaps, especially) a brilliant engineer, can read a PM's mind by reading the requirements document. The devil is in the details that must define precisely and specifically the expected functionality. The Product Manager's job is to communicate to engineering *"what"* to build. Engineering's task is then to decide *"how"* to build it.

Step 5: Confer with Engineering

Plan to spend considerable up-front time with engineering to review the high and medium priorities. The purpose of these meetings is to provide engineering with enough information to make estimates of the person-hours needed to implement each requirement. They will need to specify who has the necessary skills to complete various requirement implementation tasks since not every engineer will have the skills to tackle every requirement. It's important that engineering not only counts the hours required, but also accounts for available personnel. Along the way, as estimates are being developed, engineering may require additional information from the PM. Cutoffs, deadlines and timelines are critical in this iterative process—avoid "analysis paralysis."

Step 6: Negotiate.

Once the organization knows what can be built within the development cycle, the PM will need to adjust priorities. There may be an abundance of high priority requirements in a specific area for which engineering doesn't have the needed skills. This may gate the ability to get all requirements satisfied in one development cycle without deploying additional resources, perhaps outside the firm. Engineering estimates should factor in existing resource allocation capabilities to reveal precisely what can and cannot be done in the current cycle. Work with engineering to produce the optimal development plan. The outcome must be a reliable list of the highest priorities, perhaps sprinkled with a few medium priorities. When the requirements and development plan are ready to be signed off, engineering can then get heads-down and commence development.

Step 7: Finalize the requirements document.

At this point, the PM should return to the requirements document and note which requirements are part of the current development cycle so that (s)he can track which requirements are deferred and which are scheduled to "make this train." Don't be surprised if it takes a few cycles to get in the groove. This work is not easy and getting to know an engineering team and its capabilities requires time.

Step 8: Communicate the plan.

Once the requirements document is ready, provide a confidential summary of the plan to relevant people in the organization. Let sales, marketing and finance know what is coming in the next product release. Include a summary of features in the current release as well as the next release. If cycles are overlapped, talk about the generally available release, beta release, and next planned release. With everyone in the organization knowing what's on the horizon, the entire organization can pull together in a common direction to achieve its goals. It is a good idea to spell out the priorities for each requirement so that expectations are set in case some of the features "do not make the current train." Sales and marketing plans can be adjusted accordingly. Some organizations keep critical planning information confidential, and only allow authorized spokespersons such as the Product Manager to present the information to external audiences. Other organizations are freer in sharing their longer-term product directions in and outside of the organization. The caveat is that if future plans are discussed outside the organization, "planned features" sometimes end up in contracts on which the organization will be legally bound to deliver. Despite having an NDA, a customer that hears about a hot new feature will undoubtedly be disappointed should that feature miss the cycle and not be delivered in the planned timeframe. It is very important to manage expectations.

Step 9: Maintain the requirements document.

Continue adding new requirements into the document between cycles as new ideas or needs are uncovered. It's the little things that add up, making the Requirements Document the central repository of ideas and required actions. Before each release cycle, it will be very useful to have all that information in one place. It will save the PM a ton of time in hunting down random emails and notes.

Chapter 4: The Product Delivery Process

Winning in highly competitive markets is about three factors: execution, execution, and of course, execution. To the Product Manager, execution is the product delivery process. Good ideas can fail during implementation, meaning that great products can fail if they are not delivered properly.

The many parallel activities that happen during and after the software development cycle can make or break a product. For example:

- It is not uncommon that a product is finished from a development perspective, but issues such as order codes, installation procedures, and licensing are not yet decided.
- Documentation may not be finished in time.
- Many times, sales force personnel are trained on a new product *after* it has been launched in the marketplace.

In summary, *a software product is much more than code.* It's tempting to get so wrapped up in development and support issues that it is easy to forget about the details of product delivery—all of the activities needed to get the product ready for sale and delivery to customers. Again, here is where the Product Manager must earn his or her keep.

The process of Product Delivery can be complex due to the interdependencies and timing that must be orchestrated across multiple functions, people, and business partners. Larger companies often have well-defined product delivery processes perhaps using Stage Gate Process or other formal methods. Many assign a full-time leader, other than the Product Manager, to marshal the product delivery process. Smaller organizations require that the delivery process be scaled down so they can manage this complex process effectively. Here is one way they are doing it.

The Product Delivery Team (PDT)

The Product Delivery Process starts with a cross-functional team: The Product Delivery Team (PDT). The objective of the PDT is on-time, quality product delivery. The PDT should be made up of a representative from each function of the company: accounting, finance, engineering, distribution, marketing, sales, support and others if appropriate. Each function that is impacted by product decisions should provide a representative to the PDT. For example, deciding to separate a component and sell it as an add-on rather than embed it in the base product, will at least impact the sales department, distribution, and marketing functions.

In order to gain company-wide commitment, the PDT leader, who in smaller companies usually is the Product Manager, must interact with the functional department heads to form and launch the PDT. Each functional department will need to represent the department and drive follow-up action items to completion. While it is critical that senior management support the PDT, it is not always recommended that senior managers be the functional representatives in the PDT. The PDT is a working team of "doers" .

The PDT has three distinct goals:
1. To facilitate the delivery of new product releases in a controlled and predictable manner by building in accountability throughout the product delivery process.
2. To eliminate product delivery readiness problems before the product is released and announced.
3. To promote continuous, measurable process improvement in delivering quality, on-time products.

Using the product delivery process, companies will acquire better cross-functional communication and cooperation towards quality and control of product delivery activities.

The PDT process has four key elements: Meetings, Minutes, Checklists, and Product Business Plans.

1. PDT Meetings

Regular meetings are essential for the PDT process to establish accountability and allow for ongoing communications among members. Meetings should be scheduled at least every two weeks, for one to two hours. All members are required to participate in all meetings which means senior management buy-in to the process is critical. Ideally PDT responsibilities should be part of the job description of departmental representatives and part of their performance appraisals. Each functional department's primary representative will have an alternate to step in when the primary is unable to attend meetings or otherwise participate in the work of the PDT. Although a face-to-face meeting is the general preference, PDT meetings can include remote team members via tele or video conferencing to achieve their required participation.

The PDT Leader should prepare meeting schedules and agendas well in advance so that team members can plan and prepare accordingly. The PDT Leader should use the first meeting to ensure everyone is in sync with the rules and process of the PDT. The leader needs to explain why the PDT is important and how it will work. The team leader provides a charter document and a set of procedural rules that the team can agree to and sign off on. Sample documents are included in Appendices C and D. As with all-important product delivery documents, make these readily accessible internally so all stakeholders can review them as necessary.

Make clear to the team that the PDT is responsible for monitoring the status of the product throughout its lifecycle. This means that the PDT cannot change the software requirements or alter the development plans, but that they must focus on the delivery of the planned product.

PDT Meetings Checklist:

✓ Confirm attendance
✓ Review checklist(s) status
✓ Discuss agenda items
✓ Review existing action items
✓ Note next meeting and any future agenda items
✓ Adjourn meeting
✓ Write, distribute and post meeting minutes (within 48 hours)

2. PDT Minutes

At each meeting, the leader or a designee should take detailed minutes including general discussion of issues and action items that require additional time or outside resources to resolve. Note new action items with distinct bullets and dates. Each action item should have a "Designated Responsible Individual (DRI)"—someone accountable for getting the work done. The minutes should note from meeting to meeting if an action item is closed or is still outstanding. Once noted as completed, move action items to closed items for the next meeting minutes. This allows members to see what has been closed and what remains open at each meeting. PDT members are responsible for distributing the minutes within their functional departments as appropriate. The minutes should be archived on an intranet for company-wide reference. It is best to write and distribute PDT minutes within 48 hours after the meeting while the information is fresh in everyone's minds.

The PDT leader will rely on the minutes to keep the team focused on critical action items, those things that must get done. If an action item lingers on the minutes for too long, it's time to escalate it outside the group for resolution. Usually this won't happen if senior management has already agreed to the PDT and given the PDT members the responsibility to get the job done.

3. PDT Checklists

Creating initial PDT checklists is a difficult task and may take weeks or months to complete, but the task is well worth the effort. Checklists help ensure that essential activities don't fall through the cracks and they keep all the interdependencies organized and coordinated. A sample checklist is included in Appendix E that illustrates how one company used this instrument. Some Product Managers use tools such as Microsoft Project or other software project management packages. The goal is to manage the process and detail the timing of each activity.

However, the main thing to keep in perspective is that communication, not the tool, is the important aspect of what is being managed. Not everyone on the team will be a professional project manager or have the necessary tools to create or review plans. Consider function over form. While details are essential in describing activities, trying to assign specific times and durations can be complicated and time-consuming. Do what is right for the organization by starting as simple as possible. As the organization becomes proficient in using the checklists, more sophisticated checklists and tracking processes can be deployed.

The checklists and the timing of events must be tied back to the development process. On the sample checklist in Appendix E, the activities are timed against the Base Level Integration Plan. In this way parallel engineering and PDT tasks can be managed to ensure that dependencies are always visible and accounted for.

The best way to develop the checklist is for each PDT member to determine what they believe to be the necessary steps in his or her department as well as dependencies with other departments— no detail is too small. The more details, the more the list will reflect the actions that need to be taken to ensure on-time, quality delivery. For example, accounting may note that it needs to establish a new product number in its accounting system and review sales order forms to include the new product. Subsequently, the revised order entry system must be tested before the product is launched. A customer should not try to order the new product only to uncover problems in the order processing system. How about royalties that need to be paid to business partners that will affect how product sales are tracked and reported? How is discounting handled in the system? If the new product is part of a bundled package, can the accounting systems handle the order and properly report on it? The sample checklist provides a good start for any PDT, but keep in mind that every company is different and the checklists should be customized to fit every specific delivery process. Before the checklist is shared company-wide, the PDT leader should meet with each department representative to ensure that he or she understands his or her tasks and is accounting for all necessary steps in the delivery process charged to the functional department. The PDT representative may be unaware of tasks done by a colleague, so it is important that the entire function is represented. To this end, the PDT Leader and department manager can serve as the facilitators. Functional managers will see what the team has determined to be the process and may not agree with what they see, or they may want to simply augment the process. It's not uncommon for functional managers to be surprised by seeing their routine operations written down in black and white. Such surprises can lead to process improvements that, in turn, can lead to significant productivity improvements before the checklist is even finished.

Once solid draft checklists are completed, a PDT meeting needs to be held where team members present their lists to the group to receive feedback. There will be discussions on why some items are on each list, or that additional items need to be added to the lists. With departmental checklists completed, the PDT Leader can consolidate them into a master PDT checklist and connect interdependencies across functions. A final check with the PDT members will ensure that the consolidated list is correct. It's now time to celebrate a major milestone in the product delivery process. Make sure senior management is aware that the milestone has been achieved and encourage them to acknowledge those who contributed the critical product delivery process.

The PDT leader can now start each PDT meeting with a review of the checklist(s) and status for each activity. The PDT will need a checklist for each BLIP or version that is being worked on at any given time. The PDT will have active checklists for the product version that is currently in planning, the version that is in development, and the version that is in beta. At each PDT meeting, the PDT Leader should review all checklists and update them as necessary and make sure the checklists are always internally accessible. Appending updated checklists with PDT minutes will keep all stakeholders abreast of where things stand.

Organizations who use PDT checklists will find that over time they will continue to improve the process and update the master checklist template. This is very good because it shows that the organization is finding issues, holes, overlaps, or disconnects that can weigh down effectiveness in the product delivery process. Ideally, after every product goes into General Availability (GA), the PDT should hold a post-delivery review to discuss what went well and not so well. Adjust the master checklist as needed and note findings and actions in the minutes.

Organizations that wish to pursue International Organization for Standardization (ISO) or other quality certifications will find that the checklist and overall PDT process provide a solid foundation to build upon. The ideas behind the PDT process come from such initiatives and even without formal certification, the process can be a major selling point demonstrating how a company concretely manages quality and reliable delivery.

4. Product Business Plans (PBP)

Every product and version should have a Product Business Plan that brings together all the product information in one document containing the pertinent information about the product release. The PBP should contain general functionality information as well as environments supported, product codes, available training and services, pricing, available documentation, testing plans and so on. *A sample PBP is included in Appendix F.*

PBPs can provide a wealth of critical product information to a new employee or others outside the PDT process. A PBP is the summation of PDT decisions and information pulled into one place for anyone in the organization to reference as needed.

In smaller organizations with limited resources, creating a PBP may not be practical. If checklists and minutes of the PDT are used properly, it is possible to forego a PBP. However, as an organization grows, PBPs can provide an effective means of training new people and ensuring that critical and accurate product information is readily available throughout the organization.

In summary, the PDT and product delivery process are another main aspect of an organization's ability to deliver quality software products on time. As with any process, product delivery requires commitment from the top and execution throughout the organization. A solid delivery process can be a major selling advantage, bringing confidence to new and existing customers. As a bonus, it can be a vehicle to attract top-notch personnel who recognize the importance of a company-wide practice of superior product delivery.

Chapter 5:
The Beta Testing Process

Beta testing remains one of the most controversial parts of the software lifecycle process. In many ways, it's a necessary evil. It is necessary because ony people outside of the company can truly help validate that the software is working properly and that all aspects of the product (documentation, support, installation) are functioning well according to requirements. Beta testing is a real challenge because it requires a company to recruit external volunteers, asking them to do relatively thankless work.

Beta tests logically occur after alpha or internal testing. Once the software has been both unit and system tested by engineering, other people in the company can test it during an alpha phase. Support personnel, pre-sales and post-sales personnel are great people to involve during alpha testing. As with beta testing, the more the tests can simulate real usage of the product, the better the testing will be. This means having people install the product (if appropriate) and use the associated documentation and help facilities. If use of the new product requires upgrading an existing system, a number of important issues may be revealed. As with all issues that are identified be sure to tracked alpha issues and ensure that the issues are resolved. If the alpha test is planned within the development cycle, participants need ample notice to prepare adequately and devote enough time to the testing. This will help get decent results from the alpha stage before moving into beta.

During alpha testing, the organization should select a beta testing coordinator, ideally, a lead quality assurance person for the product. In smaller organizations, this person may have to be the PM, though this will distract the PM from focusing on other critical activities that must be accomplished during this time. The beta coordinator is responsible for identifying and selecting sites, getting plans and agreements executed, monitoring and reporting progress and issues, wrapping up, and summarizing the beta tests.

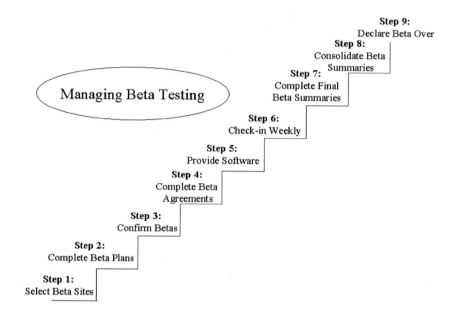

Finding and Selecting Beta Candidates

Beta testers are often power users that like to be on the cutting edge or on the "inside". Usually the PM already knows some of these people as they are most likely heavy users of customer support and other communication channels where they have access to internal people or processes. They may sometimes seem like "pains" but do work with them thankfully. They can be invaluable to a PM in identifying requirements as well as being eager beta sites.

Some Product Managers make the mistake of assuming that customers will forgive sloppiness during beta testing. Even though the software is in beta, give customers the best possible impression of the software, documentation, and related processes. Happy customers quickly become disenchanted with a problematic beta experience. Thereafter they not only shy away from doing future beta tests, but these customers may delay purchasing or upgrading to the new product. Don't go into beta until the product is ready to be showcased to customers and prospects—and be sure the internal organization is ready to respond to issues. Customers that beta test products expect extremely high levels of customer service. If they don't get it, they will stop testing and their overall impression of the software company will be negatively impacted.

There are a number of reasons why someone would be willing to beta test a product. Obvious ones include:

- Early access to functionality that the user really needs or wants.
- Free support and software is part of the deal
- The user enjoys tinkering with new things

Not so obvious reasons include:

- Customers get direct contact with product management and engineering. This gives them an inside channel going forward.
- They may want to be considered to be a "special" customer expecting special treatment in return for their efforts—"you scratch my back, I'll scratch yours".
- The potential opportunities to be in the media or recognized otherwise as experts make them feel important.

In marketing a beta program, don't shy away from pointing out all these benefits. Position beta testing as an honor and special privilege and make it clear that not everyone who wants to participate is selected. Some companies reward beta users with prizes or discounts on future product purchases. Use good judgment. If there are obvious beta sites, go to them first. If more are needed, contact customers and see if there are willing volunteers. Consider also allowing prospects to participate in the beta testing to gain a totally new perspective from people less familiar with the product. However, be sure to validate why someone outside the customer base would want to test — don't give competitors indirect access to the company's unreleased software. Also make sure that there is no risk giving a prospect a negative beta experience. However, beta testing can be used to attract prospects that haven't yet committed to buying the product. A positive experience might move them closer to a purchase decision. Work closely with the sales people in selecting both customers and prospects for beta testing.

There is no magic number of beta sites—this will depend on the size of the product and how much new functionality there is. Because no one customer will likely test the entire product, develop a Beta Test Plan that ensures all aspects of the product are sufficiently tested.

Beta Test Plans

To develop a Beta Test Plan, start by working with Engineering to decide what needs to be tested in terms of new features or capabilities. Identify which older functions should be tested to ensure that the new features added haven't adversely impacted them. Take the feature-function list and put it into a Beta Test Plan as shown in Appendix G. The test plan will guide candidate beta sites as to what needs to be tested and which tests they are expected to perform. Use the plan to talk to beta candidates about their interest in these features, and thus their interest in testing them. Work with them to go through the test plan to indicate which parts of the testing they are capable and willing to do. Each site should have its individual test plan.

Assume that half of the sites will not follow through with their commitments! This is just the nature of the beast. Things change and priorities get altered, no matter how well intentioned beta sites are. Plan for this drop-off so that comprehensive beta testing can still be achieved. Although quality, not quantity, is the real issue, plan for sufficient overlap in beta testing so that each feature is covered.

Once enough sites are recruited to cover the necessary testing, be sure to get back to the all the candidates to let them know if they have been selected for the tests. Tell rejected sites why they were not selected and let them know they may be called on again in the future.

With the accepted sites, the next step is to have them sign and return a Beta Test Agreement.

Beta Test Agreements

A Beta Test Agreement is a legal document that states that the software that is being provided is not "production ready" and frees the software company from liabilities caused by using the software. The agreement reinforces that the beta software should not be run in a production environment nor expected to be perfect. *A sample agreement is included in Appendix H for review.* Have legal counsel draft a company-specific version to use. Do not deliver or give access to software to beta sites until they have the agreement executed.

The Testing Period

Once the product is installed and beta sites are working, the beta coordinator should contact the customers at least once every week to check in and monitor progress. Issues should be documented, distributed, and followed up. Use the same software defect tracking system that has been in use throughout the development process to collect and manage all issues arising during beta testing. The system can keep engineering and other departments informed about bugs and other issues that surface to ensure that corrections are made in a timely manner. It is especially important to communicate resolved issues back to the beta sites.

Conduct regular update meetings with the product delivery team to let them know the status of beta testing and what issues, if any, need to be addressed. Keep an eye on the timeframe for testing and check to see that each site is progressing. Remember that some of the sites will fall off due to changing priorities or lack of continuing interest—that's precisely why overlap is built in to ensure there are enough test sites to carry out a complete test.

Beta Test Summaries

All stakeholders will have great interest in Beta Test Summaries that report the results of each site's tests. The template in Appendix I can be tailored and provided to each test site. The template includes a summary of what the site tested, what they found as issues, what was resolved and what is still outstanding.

The beta test coordinator provides a complete summary of all the testing to the rest of the product team. Use the same beta test template provided to the customers as a framework when creating the summary.

Some issues will still be open after beta testing has officially ended. Such issues will need to be addressed before the product team can make the final decision whether the product is ready to leave beta and ready for "general availability."

To Beta or Not to Beta

Some software companies do not feel that beta testing is of value to their development processes. The question of whether a company does or does not conduct beta testing should be a consensus decision.

Consider the overall impact of not doing a beta test. Does the organization have confidence that the internal testing processes—component, system-level and alpha tests—will provide a deep enough examination of the code, especially from an end user's perspective? Can the organization afford the additional time and resources required to carry out proper beta tests? What is the impact on customer relationships if they find relatively significant bugs or user interface issues in the product after it has shipped as a paid-for product? Does the organization know enough about how an end user actually uses the product and does it work with have real data (not demo data) to conduct tests that reflect a broad range of scenarios and "use cases"?

All of these questions are important to consider in deciding whether to do beta testing. Companies that produce enterprise-class software, as opposed to personal-use products, often work closely with a handful of customers throughout the development process. These customers can help do a modified beta where they work closely with the Product Manager or other internal personnel during the entire product release cycle. Design reviews, user interface reviews and other such activities can be face-to-face or accomplished by using webcasting to involve customers in the testing process without having to ship and install code at their sites. The overall question of beta testing should be revisited by the organization for each release cycle.

Chapter 6:
Product Launch

While a formal launch is not appropriate for every release, some launch activities should be considered for each change in the product. Either marketing or product management may be responsible for launching the product or a subsequent release. In either case, the PM must ensure that critical launch activities are addressed and thereafter (s)he can declare that the company is ready to launch the product.

The Gold Version

First and foremost, make sure that engineering has cut the final product on to permanent media—the so-called "gold" version. Final documentation and install procedures should be on the gold version and a copy needs to be escrowed per corporate policy. An escrowed product is a complete final set of software and documentation put in a safe place away from the office. There are numerous companies that provide escrow services if desired. They are typically inexpensive and provide a high level of protection for the product, ensuring that if there is some catastrophic event that destroys the computers or software within the office, there is always an emergency backup copy of the entire product available.

Make sure that the pre-sales and support teams have access to the final version by announcing how to access the software and documentation. Now is also the time to announce that the product is available to customers.

By now, the marketing team should have produced the necessary marketing materials and sales tools to reflect the new capabilities of the product. Let the internal people know where to access these new materials and make sure that they are available to customers via the sales team, the Web, or other means.

Training: Partners, Sales and Customers

Partners, customers and people in the organization who have
not already been trained during alpha or beta testing will now need
product training. Depending on the scope of the product changes,
remote techniques such as computer-based training (CBT), webcasts
or teleconferences may be used. Whether the training is remote or
face-to-face, be sure to cover the new functionality in terms of:

- How is the new version of the product now different? Is it priced
  differently? Is it packaged differently?
- How does it make the company more competitive?
- What is the impact to an existing customer that upgrades to this
  new version?

  - Does the customer require additional training? How will
    this be offered?
  - Will existing customers need to purchase any additional
    hardware or software to use the new version?
  - Will the new version impact the performance of any of the
    customer's existing systems?
  - Are there functions or tasks that an existing customer could
    do before with the older version that they will not be able
    to do now with the new version?

A Product Business Plan as discussed in Chapter 4 will be a
helpful guideline for developing training.

Demos

By now, the Product Manager should have also considered how
the product will demonstrated. It may be the PM's responsibility to
develop a demo or it may be sales, sales support or one of the other
functions. However, all companies need a demo which reflects a real
user scenario, credible data and other application aspects that can
show a potential user how the new system works. Creating this may
be quite complex and involve a lot of people. Some companies

actually treat a demo system like its very own software release, creating a requirements document and development process specific for the demo creation. Demo creation is also a major activity during product delivery and should be included in a PDT checklist to ensure it is delivered on time.

Screencasts are useful for demonstrating software features. A screencast is a digital recording of computer screen output, usually containing audio narration. Just as a screenshot is a picture of a user's screen, a screencast is essentially a movie of what a user sees on their monitor. Jon Udell of *Inforworld* came up with the term, and Camtasia Studio is one of his favorite screencast tools. Creating a screencast helps software developers show off their work. It is a useful tool for software users as well, to help report bugs, as the movie takes the place of potentially unclear written explanations, or to show others how a given task is accomplished in a specific work environment. Screencasts are excellent tools for learning how to use new software, and several podcasts have started to teach users how to use software through screencasts.

Whatever its format, a demo is a key selling tool and is a critical part of virtually every sales process. Company personnel should be trained on the proper way to demonstrate the software and ideally, an internal blog or other mechanism can be used to share best practices among field personnel.

Press Releases

Press releases are an effective means of announcing a new product and spreading the word to customers and prospects. A well written and pitched press release can help land articles and product reviews in the trade press. Press releases can also communicate to investors and other stakeholders about the company's progress.

The key to an effective press release is having a catchy headline that explains why the product release is important. Don't just announce the product and its new features. Explain why someone should be interested in this release and how it can change something about the way they or the target market works. Include a subtitle to elaborate the headline. Some of the wire services only pick up the headlines and not the subheads so it is critical that the headline conveys the key message and piques the interest of the reader. Web crawlers will pick up keywords beyond the headlines so also make sure the proper keywords are used in the release so that the search engines and other indexing systems will associate the release properly. The toughest challenge is to make press releases as short as possible.

New software product press releases should include citations from a customer or two that has beta tested the software. Quote them and describe how they are using the new product. This testimony can make a tremendous difference in how people perceive the value of the product. Customer validation is the difference between a product being perceived as "vaporware" or something real and valuable.

Be sure to get the customers' written approvals on any quotes or other references about them that are cited in the release. Make sure up front that some, if not all, of the beta testers are prepared to talk with the media, prospects, and other outsiders. Set up a protocol on who in the organization can contact the reference sites and inform the organization that any contact initiated is done only through the established protocol. This will help protect valuable references from being swamped by inquiries.

Once the release is finished, it is ready to be "wired." Essentially wiring a release means that a press release service posts the release or sends it out to their subscribers. There are many services available including Business Wire, PRWeb, PR Newswire, and Market Wire. Pricing varies greatly depending on the length of the release, the region, industry or other parameters selected. However, with some, free posting is available as a basic service. These sites typically offer add-on services that for various fees will raise the rank of a press release, increase the outbound distribution of the release and other things that increase exposure. Depnding on the objectives of posting the release, it may or may not make sense to use a free service and subsequently manually email the release to a target list.

Right after the release is wired, post a copy on the company website and distribute to the company's opt-in email lists. Where possible, personalize the emails so that the release isn't trapped in an email filter or noted as SPAM.

No press release should be issued in isolation. It should be part of an overall PR plan and used as only one vehicle for getting the word out.

David Meerman Scott's article, "The New Rules of PR" points out that press releases can be used for more than major events such as product announcements. Here is some of his advice with regards to using press releases today on the web:

- Instead of just targeting a handful of journalists, create press releases that appeal directly to buyers
- Write releases replete with keyword-rich copy
- Create links in releases to deliver potential customers to landing pages on the company's website
- Optimize press release delivery for searching and browsing
- Drive people into the sales process with press releases

Building a PR Plan

While there are entire books devoted to the activities of PR, we will just touch on its importance and some basic tactics that are relevant to the job of a PM. Since it is a critical important part of the product launch activities, every Product Manager should have a basic understanding of what it is and how PR works. Most likely, the PM will be very involved in the PR strategy and activities.

As part of an overall marketing strategy, PR serves to meet the following objectives:

1. To generate sales leads by reaching and attracting buyers.
2. To develop the company image, brand, or buzz in the marketplace.
3. To gain insight into the market that helps generate product or marketing requirements.

Chapter 7 discusses additional marketing activities that are crucial to launching and sustaining product awareness. Both the media and industry analysts can play an important role in positioning a company and product in the market. They can help generate leads and identify other business opportunities for an organization. However, if improperly managed, these channels can also create negative press about a company, so it is critical that PMs don't just jump into this activity without proper preparation.

Many public relations firms offer media training. Whether or not an agency is used, media training is essential to knowing how to work with the press and other media outlets. The training will prepare PMs and other appropriate company personnel to properly communicate information and positioning about the company and product(s). This training also helps company spokepeople to handle potentially tough or dangerous questions during an interview. Though it may seem intuitive, knowing how to conduct a successful media interview isn't as easy as it may appear. Proper training can give PMs both the information and practice needed to achieve the best possible results in all PR opportunities.

Many companies enlist the help of a PR agency to drive the overall communications strategy. An overall communications plan will include the launch deliverables and subsequent milestones. The launch may already be part of an existing communications plan, in fact. The communications plan will include the PR, materials, personnel resources, metrics and objectives critical to the success of the products (or company). Here we will focus on one of the key elements: PR.

While marketing is usually responsible for PR, they will rely on the Product Manager to participate in much of the planning and execution. A PR strategy includes at least the following elements:

- Message and positioning of the product and company.
- Available and needed materials such as brochures, presentations, and Web support that can be used to communicate the message.
- Identification of the audiences that are important to receive the message such as investors, customers, prospects, press, analysts

and employees.

- A plan for how to communicate the message to the identified audiences. This should not be a one shot communication but rather an ongoing campaign to each audience as appropriate. The campaign should include a press and analysts plan, trade show plan, direct marketing plan and other means to communicate product information.
- Identification of available personnel who are media trained and can effectively deliver the message in interviews. Having a short biography on each person will help when pitching the spokesperson to the media or for presentation opportunities.
- A media kit identifying key materials and information that can be used to follow up with media inquiries. This kit may be available in hardcopy paper, online internally or externally.
- Identification of target channels – print, TV, radio, web, associations, analysts, consultants, conferences, and so on.
- A launch plan outlining the timing of all activities that will commence with a new release of the product. Typically these activities start prior to product delivery so they may overlap or be used within a PDT checklist.

Industry Analysts

In the software market, a number of industry analyst firms offer consulting and research services to vendors and user organizations. Gartner, IDC, Forrester Research, and AMR Research are some bigger names. Tower Group and the Patricia Seybold Group specialize in vertical or technology market segments. The market changes often with mergers and new players so it is important to do research to find the influencers in a specific sector. Most of these firms publish a handful of reports that are freely available to give non-subscribers a taste of that firm's work. The majority of their reports, however, are only accessible to subscribers since this constitutes the core of the analyst firm's business. While some firms try to accommodate smaller businesses, subscriptions are typically still expensive and may lock out smaller companies from obtaining desired information and support. However, even without being a subscriber, there are many ways to productively use industry analysts to gain input into product and company positioning. Ideally the analysts will help promote the product to their constituents in writing and or through word-of-mouth. For example, a well-packaged, unique message will catch an analyst's attention and he or she will want to follow the company. Check out the analysts' writings and presentations through their companies' Web sites. If they published a report on an area related to the technology, its all the more reason to contact him or her. Remember that the analyst's job is to be an industry expert, and if a company can offer the analyst cutting edge information, it is in the analyst's best interest to keep up with that organization. Just don't be surprised by how many times the salespeople try to get a new company to become a client. After all, that is how they make a living.

To help identify key analysts, keep an eye on the media for those that get quoted in relevant publications and Web sites. Ask partners about which analysts they work with. Ask investors and customers whom they look to for industry expert opinion.

PR experts state that a target PR list (analysts, media, and other relevant influences) should be no more than 20 individuals or companies in total to be effective. More than this makes it hard to effectively research and maintain a listing of the people and their organizations and build relationships with them. The key here is to prioritize the targets and then communicate regularly with newsworthy information. Because analysts change companies and companies merge from time to time, just keeping this target list up to date can be a challenging task.

When planning to launch a new product, start the process by briefing target analysts. Consider doing this prior to the completion of beta. Analysts can later serve as helpful references for the press. Analysts like to have the inside news first so they can communicate it to their clients and remain "in the know." Use them as sounding boards along the way, if possible. In this way, they tend to be very helpful and when it comes time to publicly announce the software, they will already be experts on the product and the company. Many analyst firms, however, will only allow an annual briefing to non-subscribers. If this is the case, be sure to plan the one meeting so it coincides appropriately with the product launch plans.

Most analysts are astute and have in-depth knowledge of the industry. Remember, though, that the analysts are interested in new, relevant information. Be careful not to assume, however, that they know every acronym and are familiar with all related technologies. Prepare for meetings by researching the analyst's background and any recent reports or presentations that the analyst has done. This will indicate his or her areas of concentration and interests. Try to get feedback throughout discussions and don't hesitate to ask for their opinion about the product, business, and strategy—they love to provide their perspectives.

Media List

Magazines, ezines, radio, TV, Blogs, wikis, and newspapers are channels to consider in a PR strategy. They all require both proactive and reactive media relations. Proactive media relations mean pushing out new information out to media in hopes of gaining their attention. Activities such as a press release or other unsolicited content sent, a telephone or in-person briefing, or other marketing promotion can all be part of a proactive media strategy. Reactive PR fulfills the media's already stated information needs published in editorial calendars. These calendars are usually available on the media's Web site or by calling their respective advertising departments. Offer an article or an expert for the topics they plan on covering.

To start building a media plan, the first step is to create a target list of the people, publications or web sites, and firms that are desired to be reached. There are various Web services and software tools that can be purchased to help identify these targets. Alternatively, the research can be done manually using the Web to do a basic search for publications in the market space. Many industry publications offer free subscriptions or online versions that can be used to evaluate if there is a good fit. For each media outlet, obtain information about each magazine's subscriber base including demographics, job titles, and purchase influence. This information will help determine if the readership is a good match. A senior level magazine probably won't publish details of a new product version unless it is included in a user story or some other more benefit-oriented format. The more known about a target publication and its readers, the better it can be pitched by catering to their style and subscriber interests.

Once the media list is built, plan the kinds of information that will be communicated. Communications will include a mix of press releases, presentations, emails, telephone calls, meetings, and product demonstrations. Reactively, review the editorial calendars and contact the magazines well in advance of their deadlines to offer relevant information. Send reminders to them every few weeks so they don't forget about the available expert or content as they get closer to working on that topic. Keep close track of each person contacted and record any follow up activity required. Always follow up! PR is truly all about sales, so assume multiple calls and contacts need to be made. Track everything carefully and have patience.

Keep the media list fresh by validating the editorial contacts and audience demographics every few months. Understand if the content for that media channel is staff or freelance driven. Get very familiar with the media channel and continually look for news or other trends that help make the information relevant and timely.

Submit article proposals or already completed articles to the media. Never write an article that's specific to a product. Instead, write articles about a technology area and mention the company as an example of one vendor in that space. Another approach is to submit a user story about a customer using the product, or better yet, let a magazine write an article in which they can work with a customer. Of course, give the customer a heads up and prep them on the key messages. Be sure to follow up with the writer after the interview to see if they require any additional information. Ask when the article is expected to go out.. Keep this information in the contact tracking so a copy of the article can be tracked down once it is published. Some media will insist on exclusivity of any content used. Be sure to understand this before handing over the article. Ideally it is great to reuse the same content in different places but it may be worth the sacrifice if one of the key target channels requires exclusivity. Be sure to track when and where each article was published.

Numerous clipping services will scan the media on a regular basis to keep clients abreast of their media placements. A set of keywords including a company name, product name, competition and other such things tells the service what they should track. When submitting this keyword list, be sure to include all variations in names to capture all instances. These services are not very expensive and can work with print and online publications. Google now even provides an alert service (Google Alerts) that will continuously look for web entries with any number of keywords identified. A collection of media mentions is one way to validate whether the PR strategy is working or not. Ultimately a successful PR campaign will drive leads and sales with a targeted and actual ROI achieved.

With a new product launch, both analysts and press will want to talk with beta sites. Manage this activity so that the customers don't get overwhelmed. As mentioned previously, assign a protocol for this to keep it clear who and how these sites can be contacted. Let the sites know when and to who their names are given to so that they can expect a reference call. A heads-up in these situations is always appreciated and, more importantly, it will save everyone from unpleasant media surprises. Brief the sites in advance and try to provide them insight about the analyst's or media's specific interests. Note a particular company and product message that ideally they should help reinforce. Follow up with the analysts after reference calls to see if additional information is needed.

When communicating with the external community, be sure to keep messages simple and tight. Boil the news down to one or two main points and keep information focused on the benefits of the new software, rather than on individual features. Apply the "who cares" rule so that every statement of fact will have value to the analysts and press and, in turn, their audiences of readers or clients. Analysts will probably be in tune with technology and terms of the trade, while the media most likely needs more easily explained information so that they can readily communicate it forward without being experts in that area themselves. Providing both types of audiences with written materials that they can use directly or "cut and paste" is very helpful. This not only saves them time but also avoids possible interpretation errors. Always offer them to review drafts and don't be afraid to ask them what they will be writing about or doing with the information provided. Ask them how the announcement might affect their clients or readers. This opens the opportunity to position the announcement in the company's terms rather than leave it for the media to figure out on their own. Ask if there are other things that will assist them in understanding and communicating the benefits of the new product.

Track briefings and the analysts' work so results can be shared with colleagues, partners and customers. If there has already been consistent and respectful communication with the media and analysts, the launch should be easier since the media can focus on the news and not get bogged down with the history of the company and its overall product offerings.

Post Mortem Launch Review

Do a "post-mortem" review of the launch to identify areas that went well and those that did not. Continuous improvement of all product-related activities should be everyone's goal and hopefully encouraged by the company's senior management. The more a company provides positive reinforcement for employees during post-mortem reviews, the more they will realize improvements from cycle to cycle.

Launch Party

A final but important "task" for a good product launch is to celebrate. Get the entire company together to toast the success of the new product and thank all those who made it possible. This opportunity to recognize the achievements of the team will reinforce creativity, enthusiasm, and hard work for the future.

Chapter 7: Product Marketing

Some people have the misconception that "anyone can do marketing." Perhaps their reasoning is that unlike engineering where bad code will simply not work, bad marketing isn't as obvious. Like any other business discipline, however, product marketing requires knowledge, experience, scientific methods, and metrics.

Although some companies distinguish product marketing from corporate marketing or brand marketing, product marketing includes the activities necessary to identify, acquire, foster, and retain customers for a specific product. Activities include finding new sales prospects, helping to support cross-selling and up-selling products to new or existing customers, expanding existing customer relationships, and building brand loyalty. Whether placing advertisements, attending tradeshows, or sending out direct mail, the ultimate goal is to acquire and retain profitable customers.

Regardless of which functional department actually does the marketing, the Product Manager must be actively involved in the marketing of the product. Ideally, the Product Manager will not actually *do* the marketing, for it requires an objectivity that is hard to strip away from the PM as "the product champion." Additionally, the Product Manager will be busy with all the tasks described in this book! However, because the PM has the knowledge and influence to help position the product, he or she should be deeply involved with the marketing plans and their execution. The PM must support the marketing initiatives and communication efforts.

Positioning

Positioning defines the market segments to be served by the product and communicates what the product promises to do for its buyer. Positioning is easier said than it is done. It is helpful to use focus groups and as much competitive intelligence as possible. A good exercise to help position the product is to create a personality or persona for the product itself. This exercise is called personification. Working with the marketing team, brainstorm to select a celebrity or other commonly known individual that would make a good spokesperson for the product. That is, someone who represents the attitude and qualities that match the desired impression of the product. End the personification session with a list of characteristics that describe the product. Personifying the product can help test whether the words, colors and other communication aspects fit the desired image. To ensure that the product stands out from the other offerings in the market, begin the positioning activities before and during product development. Early positioning work can influence product requirements decisions and impact product readiness determinations. Conduct formal positioning reviews for each product cycle to account for changes in the product and market. To position the product correctly, solid answers are needed for the following questions:

1. Why is the product unique?
2. What benefit(s) does it bring to the people who use it? What happens if they don't use it?
3. Who else will benefit from the product other than the direct users? What happens to them if the product is not used?
4. What other products are available that compete directly or indirectly with the product? Are there other things customers will need to spend money on that may compete with monies available for the product? Remember to appeal to potential users as well as people who may not use the product directly but have purchasing authority such as CFO or CEO.
5. Are there other ways for potential customers can achieve the same results if they don't use the product? Why would someone choose the product over the other means?
6. What kinds of people will use the product? What kinds of people buy the product? Are they creative or mathematical thinkers? What other products appeal to them and how are those products positioned?

7. How does this product complement or compete with the company's existing products?

It is possible that every market or micromarket will require unique product positioning. Be sure to consider each targeted vertical market, each individual buyer or influencer in the purchase cycle, as well as other variables that may affect positioning such as size of the prospective company and number of competitors in each market. If necessary, create and implement different positioning for each market but be wary of the limited resources in the company to support this highly targeted marketing approach.

Product Naming and Logos

Don't get too creative with the name. People will want to know what the name or logo means and an effective name will help customers remember the product if the name is easy and meaningful. Though potentially expensive, hiring a professional naming firm to select a product name and a design firm to render a logo can help. Be sure the firm has sufficient experience in the same or a similar field and that they have good track records with other products. Make sure it is clear what work will be charged for, including review cycles and initial research. Also be sure to have a clause in the contract that makes them liable for any competitive or other claims against the work. Don't get left holding the bag for a logo or name that wasn't properly researched or worse yet, copied from someone else. Of course, make sure the URL is available and consider registering many variants of the name to prevent competitors from "hijacking" the name and attracting potential prospects that accidentally type in an incorrect spelling. Also, just because the URL is available (or not), don't assume that the name isn't registered to someone else.

With a logo, decide if both a company and product logo are needed. Having two logos can be confusing. The idea of a logo is to give someone a graphical representation with which to associate a specific thing – either a company or product. Repeated visual contact is key to maintaining desired associations. If there is both a company and product logo, the audience's minds are split, making the audience work twice as hard to achieve the mental connections.

Colors can make a big difference too. If the logo is the same color as another competitor or partner, it may fail to stand out when the logo appears side by side with others. Take the opportunity to select colors and styles that really do stand out in the specific market. Beware that some color combinations can be offensive in different cultures so be sure to review the selections with as many people as possible, particularly those in or from other countries.

A professional designer that specializes in logo development can be of great help. Review his or her previous work and make sure that the style reflects the spirit of the new product and company. A good logo designer will have a process to get inside the product's or company's positioning and fully understand what is trying to be conveyed via the new logo. As with the product name, people will want to understand the significance of the logo so don't get too wild. A logo can add to an audiences' ability to recall the product name simply by seeing the logo (e.g. Microsoft's Windows or Adobe's Acrobat). Simpler designs are easier to translate into the many ways logos get used: within the software itself, in printed materials, the Web, promotional items or tradeshow giveaways (e.g. pens, hats, and writing pads. A good logo designer will render the logo in black and white, one or two PMS colors, and if desired, a full four-color rendering. Keep in mind that each color adds to the cost of printing or reproducing the logo on most non-electronic media. A logo should be identifiable in one color for the times where that is all that can used or afforded. Be sure to see how the logo looks in a reverse field where the logo is white against a color background. This will give full flexibility to use the logo while maintaining its integrity as a distinct symbol.

Some designers will want to retain certain rights to the work they produce. If they insist, find another designer. It is critical that the company, not the designer, owns the work outright and that it has the rights to alter and sell the work if it so chooses—this must be part of the designer's contract - is not an option. This is referred to as "work for hire". The company is paying for the work and resulting logo design and therefore it is the company's property to do with it as it wishes.

Be sure to get final paper and electronic copies of the logo in color and black and white. For hardcopy, get the logo printed clearly on a white background. For electronic copies, be sure to get the work in its original software format (usually Illustrator or Corel) along with any relevant .jpeg, .gif, .tif, .eps and .bmp versions of the logo - all with appropriate resolutions for the Web and print uses. An experienced designer will be familiar with these requirements and should provide these files before final signoff.

Trademarks

Whether the product name is going to be filed as a trademark or not, be sure to do a legal search on the name selected. The federal Patent and Trademark Office (PTO) offers a Web site (www.uspto.gov) where a free search of registered and pending product names by trademark class can be done. An Intellectual Property (IP) attorney can also assist with this activity. The search will indicate if anyone already owns the name or anything like it. The company can be sued for infringement if the name causes any possible confusion in the marketplace with another company that owns the name. After clearing the legal search, decide whether or not it makes sense to trademark the product name or logo. The trademark process can be time consuming and costly. Be prepared to file many different applications for different classes of trademarks, including those required in different countries—fees will vary and change every so often. Remember to account for attorney's fees in the trademark budget.

Trademarks can take several months or sometimes years to register (®), but they can immediately be displayed with a pending trademark symbol (™) even before an application has been filed. Police the mark and be prepared to oppose or sue others for possible infringement – again, realize that these activities are time-consuming and expensive. There are firms that will look out for possible infringement by other companies. The intellectual property (IP) attorney should be able to identify good watchdog services.

As the product becomes successful and gains name recognition, trademark protection can be very important. Without expending the effort, someone else could register the trademark and force the company to either pay for the use of the trademark or surrender its use, negating the hard-earned name recognition the company has in the market.

Patents

Always consider patenting the technology used inside the product. Similar to the trademark process, acquiring a patent requires an initial search for like inventions, filing a patent application, and once granted, policing and defending the patent. Patents, however, require substantially more time and money to acquire and defend than trademarks. The process requires that all of the inventors participate in the development of the patent application. An IP attorney will work with the inventors to accurately represent the product in written, "patent-ese" form. Expect this process to take a minimum of several months to accomplish. Patents are granted several months or more typically, years after application. Despite these issues, a patent will provide the same benefits of protection as does a trademark. However, the stakes are indeed higher. With a trademark, while there may be some payment penalty by the competitor for any damages caused by an infringement, the competitor can always change the product's name. If they are infringing on a patent, most likely they will have no other choice but to remove the product from the market.

Police for Consistency

The most important aspect of branding is consistency. As product champion, make sure people represent the trademarked name and logo accurately. To help police the use of the logos and name, publish a style guide that specifically describes the proper use of the logo and name. For example, if the name is to be represented using all capital letters, make sure this is noted as the proper use. When representing the logo, colors shouldn't be close, they should match exactly to the PMS or process color mix that has been selected. Anytime people alter the logo or name, there is a risk of losing the opportunity to imprint the brand on the target audience.

Don't jeopardize a trademark's effectiveness by not using it correctly. Use the logo and name proudly and as frequently as possible. When talking with customers, media or others, use the name itself rather than referring to it as "the product." When writing, use the product name often and, if possible; use the logo to provide a visual representation that reinforces the words.

Lead Generation

As noted before, marketing has one and only one overarching goal—acquiring loyal, profitable customers. Being the first step in customer acquisition, generating well-qualified sales leads is paramount. A company's existing customers represent the most cost-effective source of sales leads. Acquisition costs for new customers are five times that of acquiring new product sales from existing customers.

A multitude of marketing programs can be used to generate qualified leads, including: trade shows, advertising, direct mail, telemarketing, email, Web sites, blogs, wikis, webcasts, seminars, podcasts, public relations (PR), and Investor Relations (IR). Marketing's job is to determine the best mix of these and other channels to reach the highest number of leads.

To determine which prospects represent the greatest lead potential, do not forgo rigorous marketing research to answer such questions as:

- What demographics or other characteristics describe the best fit between prospects and the product?
- How do prospect categories or market segments compare in demand to the new product?

What are the best ways to find and attract high-priority prospects?

Finding complete answers to these questions requires much effort and rigor. Smaller companies may not have the resources to utilize sophisticated marketing research. However, more and more customer relationship management (CRM) technologies are being commoditized, thus coming within reach of small and medium-sized businesses. These products can provide a number of capabilities including:

- Segment and Campaign Management – enable users to determine and select appropriate prospects and to track the sales results before and after a marketing campaign
- Look-a-like and Propensity Modeling – allows users to identify high potential prospects using data common to the best customers. Results can be used to identify the best product matches for new and existing customers by analyzing the demographics of the customers who buy each product.
- Visual and Psychographic Profiling – by using demographic and behavioral data and geographic information, users can understand the location and preferences of their customers and prospects as part of the overall segmentation analysis
- Analytics – provide sophisticated statistical analyses to help understand patterns in large amounts of data. For example, one

could determine why customers tend to attrite or how purchase channels such as the web affect product choice.

While the costs of in-house marketing research or in-house CRM software may be prohibitive, service bureaus, consulting firms, and business process outsourcers can be tapped.

With all the resources that can be marshaled together to carry out marketing research, it's vital that the PM (or product marketing manager) define target segments as narrowly and precisely as possible. The more the company knows about the prospects, the better it can appeal to each segment's needs. CRM technologies allow some companies to segment down to a "market of one," allowing each customer's ever-changing needs and buying patterns to be recognized and met by profitably cross-selling the appropriate customized solution for each specific segment's needs.

With marketing research in hand, it's time to carefully select the mix of programs that will be used to bring in the necessary leads. By understanding the selling cycle for each market channel or segment, set goals for what kind and how many leads need to be generated. Goal setting will depend on several factors, for example, what does the sales department consider to be a qualified lead? Is it someone who has budgeted money or someone who is already evaluating competitive offerings? How many qualified leads will it take to close one sale? With answers to these kinds of questions, calculate how many leads are needed, by timeframe, for each channel and sales representative. For example, if there is a single representative in the Northeast and there are 10 trade shows planned for that area, it is possible to generate over a thousand leads for that one representative. As a result, it might be better to balance programs in other geographies or work with sales management to ensure that other sales reps can assist in following up.

Whether a marketing program is initiated by the marketing department or the sales channel, follow up if the key to success. Follow up is where most lead generation efforts break down and the single most common source of failure occurs—great marketing programs, lots of leads, but anemic follow up.

Follow up is what turns leads into sales or can help better qualify prospects. Information derived from either outcome is valuable, allowing the company to learn how to improve its lead generation activities and the product. Automated lead tracking systems are increasingly important and becoming more affordable for small and mid-sized companies. These systems help track and manage leads and provide metrics so that they can measure the efficiencies in marketing and sales programs. Automated systems can free a PM to focus on helping to find more qualified leads, while worrying less about leads falling through the cracks. Even in a very small company with the only available tool being a spreadsheet, leads can still be tracked manually as long as the company adheres to a systematic lead management process. Know where leads are coming from, who is getting them, and what are they doing to follow up. Track how long it takes to move leads to different stages of the sales cycle and what is helping close leads into deals or lost sales. The more that can tracked and measured, the better lead generation and follow-up processes can be improved which will ultimately optimize resources and generate more business.

Sales Support

Even the best Product Manager can't run the business single-handedly. As the product champion, help others become experts and provide the knowledge and tools they need to make the sale themselves, as independently as possible. Determine who needs to know what. Sales people will need to understand what the product does, whom it was designed for and how it is positioned. Do they need to understand how the product works internally or can they rely on others such as sales support personnel to impart in-depth product knowledge? Some personnel may need to know how to install and implement the product while others will be concerned about the pricing and how to justify or compare it with competitive products to a prospect. Therefore it is important to understand the unique needs of the internal audiences and design tools and information appropriate for their specific needs.

The Product Manager will be called on to educate other people with presentations, written materials, and other communication means. Expect to be brought into critical sales cycles as the expert to talk directly with customers and prospects. Often a sale is made on the efforts and enthusiasm of the Product Manager in explaining, rather than selling, to the prospect.

With help from sales and marketing, develop the necessary sales tools and make them accessible preferably on an intranet. Sales tools may include configuration and pricing aids, system requirements, brochures, and other collateral such as presentations and letter templates. Be sure appropriate people are trained on how to use the tools and listen to feedback and ideas on improving the information.

Remember that the Product Manager may be the product expert, but the salespeople who are interacting with customers regularly are the selling experts. Both parties have relevant knowledge to bring to bear on how to best sell the product. A good measure of how salespeople perceive Product Management's expertise will be how often they invite the Product Manager to participate in sales cycles. If the internal colleagues don't call, it might be that they don't view the Product Manager as helpful in their selling efforts—a great Product Manager will call to find out why!

Don't forget about people in accounting and customer support. Be sure they have the appropriate understanding of the product and related processes. Because we already know that a software product is more than programming code, be sure that everyone in the organization has appropriate product and positioning information necessary to get the job done. Anyone can help spread the word at social events, professional organizations and other venues that present an opportunity to promote the product.

The 4 P's of Marketing

The classic 4 P's of marketing are product, price, position and place (distribution). Sometimes distribution can be everything, as it dictates the structure of the company as well as product design and market segments to be reached. For example:

- Will the company rely on direct sales representatives that work for the company or will it look to partners to sell the product?
- How will partnering affect the pricing, support and future cross-sales opportunities?
- Will the product be available for sale on-line?
- Does it require a shrink-wrapped license or does it require more elaborate contracts?
- What is branded and by whom?
- Who owns the customer?

These are all key questions that need to be answered as part of a distribution strategy. The goal is to have answers long before the product is developed or specified. These answers can have a dramatic effect on every aspect of the product lifecycle.

Having covered three of the four P's of marketing, an entire chapter is needed to provide an analysis of the fourth P, pricing.

Chapter 8: Pricing

While pricing most obviously can determine the profitability and possibly the overall success of the product, pricing also positions the product. As such, pricing is a strategic decision as well as a tactical one. Pricing inevitably defines the customer base, the competition and sales process.

Pricing a product requires the ongoing evaluation of pricing assumptions and prior conclusions. Pricing, like requirements development, is as much of an art form as it is a science. Several practical considerations make up the rationale for pricing decisions.

The 4 C's of PriCCCCing

While there are 4 "P"s of marketing, there are 4 C's of pricing: *Cost, Competition, Customers and Change.*

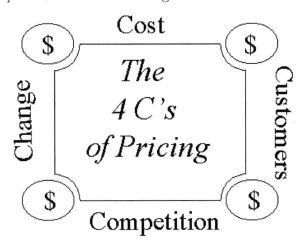

Cost

First, consider cost, the most objective variable to determine. Calculate the expenses accumulated when developing, delivering, marketing, selling, and supporting the product. Include such factors as royalties, opportunity costs, and costs of ownership. Cost of ownership (COO) (sometimes referred to as Total Cost of Ownership or TCO) includes all of the expenses a customer will accrue by using the software. Costs include ongoing maintenance fees, hardware, other software required to run the package, training, additional personnel, and so on. With a hosted application (aka Software as a Service – SaaS), the costs of providing the hosting service can be quite complex and must be determined for each installation. COO is the most effective way to compare two different systems as it better reflects the overall costs of the new system.

If possible, let the finance department lead this exercise. Finance should be able to provide related expense data for each product activity and help establish expected margins after variables such as cost of sales and royalties. The more accurately they can determine the true cost of the product, the better a price can be justifed.

Use this equation to help identify one possible price or price range for the product and related services:

Price= [Overall Product Cost / Forecasted number of units]* (1+Margin)

For example, if estimated lifetime costs are $1,000,000 and 1,000 units are projected to be sold at a 20% margin, the price calculation is $1,200.

Competition

Now compare the price with that of the competitions'. Try to assess, apples-to-apples, what the competition charges for the same product in the same sales circumstances. Don't compare a standalone product with the same component bundled into a larger package. For example, if it is a word processing application, compare it to Microsoft Word but consider the fact that most people purchase and use WORD in conjunction with the complete MS Office suite. The bundled package significantly changes the pricing, installation, and use of the individual application.

Factor in discounting practices and overall lifetime cost of ownership and maintenance for the product. Should the product be perceived as the premier offering in the market (e.g. Cadillac, Mercedes) or the value priced, economy offering (e.g. Kia, Toyota)? Think about the desired and perceived position in the marketplace and try to find the price that will position the product appropriately.

Become a "detective" or hire a consultant to help determine the competitors' pricing. Consider purchasing the competitors' products to ensure a truly accurate measure of the same elements. However, where this isn't possible, use competitive intelligence to try to determine competitive pricing. Industry analysts can help provide competitive intelligence about how various vendors are perceived in the market.

Customers

Customers and prospects are valuable sources that can provide insight into the price elasticity of a product. Informally, ask them how much they think the product is worth:

- Does the product increase their productivity or reduce their employee costs? Can they quantify this?
- Do they feel they'll get a great deal and significant value from the product? Can they quantify this?

Web casts and focus groups can be used to gather pricing input. Try to avoid "group think," and ask detailed questions about what participants would pay for that specific product. Ask if a lower price would help avoid some of the purchasing approval cycles and shorten the sales cycle? How much is that worth to both companies?

The same products offered by different companies may be priced completely differently. One vendor may "get away" with charging higher prices simply because there is a perceived added value from that particular vendor. That premium demonstrates the power of *branding*. People will pay the extra money feeling that the brand name is reputable and that the company will stand behind the software. Just as it makes a difference with ketchup or toilet tissue, it also makes a big difference in software decisions. A bad software decision can ruin careers so a reputable brand can be the comfort that prospects need to feel that others can't be wrong.

Some companies can charge premium prices because they include complementary products and services or they have superior support. Remember that a product is indeed more than software, and customers are willing to pay more to be sure they will be successful using the product.

Rather than competing on perceived quality, a product can be positioned as the "low-cost alternative." In some industries, there are ways to calculate the amount that a customer will pay for that product by estimating the target share of overall planned IT spending. The IT spending numbers can be derived from analyst reports that forecast spending on specific technologies. With further analysis, it is possible to determine a price range for the offering, or at least validate that the price is affordable for the specific marketplace.

Change

Setting prices can involve sophisticated scientific processes and analyses, but in the end, pricing almost always relies on subjective judgment. Taking input from the four C's can help support the judgment and allow the experienced Product Manager to choose an appropriate price from the start. Pricing, on the other hand, is not a static, one-time event. Market prices should be continually monitored and if necessary, the pricing structure will need to change to accommodate market changes.

Perhaps costs change or a company's needs change in terms of margin or overall ROI objectives. To bring change into perspective over the lifecycle of a product, consider the "Technology S Curve" where, in the initial stages of adoption, new technology can be priced at a premium, while later in its life, commoditization or obsolescence steps in, forcing prices downward. In the early stages of a product life cycle, early adopters will pay a premium for the innovation. Although a premium pricing strategy may be used early in the game, be ready to alter as necessary to support long-term objectives. Monitor the price throughout the product lifecycle to optimize the company's market share, profit and sales cycle goals. There simply isn't any such a thing as "the right price." In the end, pricing boils down to "the price is the best possible one for now."

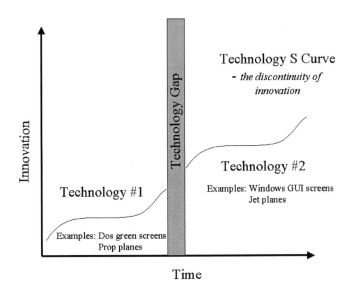

Licensing Versus Leasing

Software vendors that license software to their customers, provide them with perpetual ownership of the software product. The customer then uses the product directly or might outsource its operation to an Internet Service Provider (ISP). The customer, however, owns the software and is limited to the license terms of the software vendor.

In addition to an outright purchase of a software product, leasing has been a common arrangement since the early days when mainframe computers were the only source of business automation. With a lease, the customer doesn't own the software, just the right to use it by paying monthly or yearly fees. To terminate a lease, the user needs to return the media containing the product and present proof that usage has ceased. The leasing model provides recurring revenue for software companies and is still used to this day.

What's new with leasing arrangements today is that the user company may not even use the product in-house, on its own computers. The Internet gave rise to Software as a Service (SaaS) or hosted implementations. In this scenario, customers access the software via the Internet, leasing the vendor's hardware and networking equipment as well as the software. In some cases, the customer actually owns the hardware that is operated by an ISP/ASP (Application Solution Provider) through managed services and co-location.

Whatever the contractual arrangement, the ISP/ASP essentially provides access to the software with appropriate data storage and security. The ASP doesn't develop software products, but rather houses and operates them making them available through highly reliable and economical Internet access.

Typical ASP contracts are 2-5 year agreements that allow customers to minimize their outlays of money and resources needed for new systems. While the reduced costs and hassles are indeed attractive and very popular, some companies are still leery of using critical software that they cannot control themselves and that houses their information at a third party.

Software Pricing Models

In the software business, there are many pricing models. New ones are created to provide creative means for selling software and ensuring value to the customer. Some of the more popular models in current use include:

- *Per User/Named User* – This is one of the most common pricing models, especially with PC-based products. This model licenses one individual with a single software copy and prohibits the use of it by any other user. Users typically have unlimited use of the product. Multi-user licenses are also commonly available to allow multiple people to access and use the software. However, when using this model, users are specifically named rather than allowing a pool of users as provided with concurrent licensing.

- *Concurrent Users* – This provides a number of available licenses to be used at any one time by multiple, unspecified people. This "floating" license allows a number of people to share the software as long as only the licensed number is using it at any given time. This model is typical with server-based software products. Most concurrent licenses do not limit the amount of time or use of the product beyond the number of simultaneous users.

- *Usage* – Modeled after the notion of a utility, this pricing strategy supports the idea of "pay for what you use." For example, paying for the amount of time on the Internet is a usage price versus paying a flat fee for unlimited use which is more of a per user model. Measuring usage can be tricky. It may be possible to measure based on time or effect (e.g., number of database records, and hits per page). Another way to measure usage is estimated or perceived value to the customer. For example, the price for software designed to help doctors manage their patients' records might be based on the number of patients they serve—doctors with many patients pay incrementally more for the software. Another example is basing the price of the product on the revenue of the customer. In banking, for example, many products are priced based on the asset size of the institution. Asset size denotes the amount of money the bank manages so it directly indicates the size of the institution and an estimate of its usage.

- *System Based* – Used mostly in the database market, this pricing ties the license to a specific type of hardware or subsystem. Vendors price their products based on the kind of processor (CPU) that the software will run on. As the hardware is upgraded (or downgraded), the software license and subsequent price expands (contracts) as well. Be careful with this pricing model, as it makes it easy to penalize customers for upgrading their systems or infrastructure. A system upgrade usually improves performance and customer satisfaction so don't discourage an upgrade because of pricing.

- *Site/Enterprise License* – This pricing model provides the entire customer site with unlimited use of the software. Many software vendors use this option to generate up-front revenues and reduce the administrative costs of the licensing.
- *Value Based* – The concept of value-based pricing is to derive a relative measure of the value of the product to the customer. Some companies price their software based on the cost savings they can demonstrate—or the increased revenues generated by their software. While this model is attractive to customers, it is often very difficult to measure and monitor.
- *Combination* – Many software companies combine any two or more of these models while formulating their pricing strategies. For example, some products combine a per-server and per-user pricing model.

If the software product will be a part of a bundle or suite, additional pricing factors must be considered. Software suites combine multiple individual applications that share a common installation and share relationships among themselves. While there is synergy created by suites in providing more functionality than the individual parts, most suites are priced lower than the sum of the pieces, encouraging people to buy the whole package as opposed to only some of the parts. On the other hand, some modules in the suite do not apply to everyone but have high value for some customers. Consider charging for those modules separately to earn a premium without penalizing the rest of the customers.

Sometimes software is sold as a loss leader to encourage follow-on purchases. If the product requires services or other components for its optimal use, there is an option to give away the initial software. AOL is a classic example of this strategy, giving away its software to attract users to its services. It also gives away the service for a period of time to "hook" users.

Consider a variety of upgrade and add-on paths when deciding on the packaging and price of products. Also don't forget about prerequisite software needed to run a given product. It may make sense to consolidate some or all of that product mix and provide it as part of a single offering to reduce the complexity from a customer's perspective. This strategy may add to the cost and subsequently the price, but it is a common practice to ensure high customer satisfaction.

Also, consider the cost for a customer to switch from one product to another. If a prospect has a high switching cost to go from their current solution to the new product, perhaps provide incentives for changing products much like the telephone companies often do to get customers to change from a competition's service. Once they become customers, it may be possible to charge a higher fee simply because those customers have no choice but to continue using the product.

One last important consideration is whether the product supports critical industry or proprietary standards. For customers that want standard-compliant solutions, premium pricing may be used if this product is the only one that supports the standard. In the early stages when standards are just coming to market, use this as a pricing advantage. However, as that standard becomes more commonplace, the commoditization will then dramatically lower switching costs— with the goal of making switching costs obsolete. Depending on where the product fits in the life cycle of the developing standard, understand how standards compliance can be used as an advantage or if it is simply a necessary feature of the product offering. In addition to the software license, most products come with additional services such as installation, training, support and maintenance. These components need to be priced appropriately and integrated into the overall pricing strategy for the product.

Installation or Set-up Pricing

If the product is not a hosted solution, and there is some type of installation required, an installation price needs to be determined. Installation pricing is usually a flat fee but can vary based on the size of the installation project or overall size of the license. Some vendors charge on a time and materials basis (T&M), the same approach a mechanic takes when working on a car. T&M pricing typically includes a "not to exceed" maximum. Because it is not entirely predictable, T&M is the least appealing model to the customer. However, for the vendor, it allows them to cover unexpected environmental issues or those issues caused by the customer's failure to perform required tasks or provide required resources.

For hosted solutions, a set up fee is usually charged to cover the time of the vendor setting up a new account or customizing the application for the customer. Usually there is a fixed fee for set up but like installation, many vendors opt to include this in the overall price of the software simply to keep the pricing proposal as simple as possible.

Training Pricing

Training customers on the new software is a critical success factor for many software products. Training can take a number of forms. If delivered in person, it can be done at the customer's site, the vendor's site, a partner's site, or a rented site. Training can be priced using T&M, a fixed price, based on the number of participants, or as a percentage of the software license. Training can also be delivered via the Internet (e.g. webcasting, podcasting), using paper-based materials, or computer-assisted instruction. Pricing for these methods varies with the medium.

Training may be bundled with the product and offered by the company or a channel partner. There may be one course or a series of classes that can be taken in pieces. Consider if there should be special new customer training and then advanced training courses for more experienced users. The customer's first impression of the new software will no doubt be a reflection of his or her satisfaction with the training, so plan the training well.

Maintenance Pricing

Maintenance service refers to two things, ad hoc support and maintenance releases. Ad hoc support can be delivered through channels such as the call center, email, eChat, self-service via the Web, or a combination thereof. Context sensitive help or other embedded help services with in the product are often available to the users. Live support may be restricted to certain times such as business hours, total number of hours used, or other parameters.

Maintenance (aka dot or point) releases refer to the smaller releases of a product that address bugs or add minor functionality. The dot or point refers to the naming convention of most software products. For example, V1.2 means major release or version 1, the second minor release of that version. The "2" is referred to as the dot or point. It is common to include maintenance releases in an overall service package and to have these releases easily accessible and applied for existing customers. This helps reduce calls to the support center

Pricing for a new version upgrade to a new version is usually a fraction of the regular product's full price. However, there are many scenarios where it is in the company's best interest to upgrade all or part of its customers for free. Some vendors also include major releases or versions in their maintenance support contracts. Major upgrades may also require additional installation and training services to accompany them. As with any pricing exercise, determine the price in a holistic manner so it is acceptable when all the required products and services are bundled together.

Other Services Pricing

Many software products command an array of complementary services such as consulting that will enable a customer to better use the software. For example, Customer Relationship Management (CRM) providers offer business process analysis and strategic goal alignment services to ensure that the software is being deployed appropriately to the organization's specific needs. Services can provide lucrative means to increase revenues associated with the product line, but represent a different kind of business than that of offering a software product. Identify the complementary services that are (and should be) offered by the company and its partners. Bundle services to offer a competitive solution and increase the value of the products to customers. If it makes sense, bundle some services with the software as a way to ensure a successful implementation.

Pricing Tips

In pricing software products, a handful of critical factors should be kept in mind:

1. *Keep it simple.* It is easy to get too creative with pricing and end up with a price that is more difficult to explain than the software itself. This will cause more time and training for salespeople and cause delays in the sales cycle. Make sure pricing can be easily measured and monitored if it is based on usage.

2. *Make sure pricing decisions can be defended.* If priced well above competitors, ensure that the overall positioning and perceived value are in line with the premium price. Ensure that internal colleagues, in particular salespeople, understand how and why the price is the way it is.

3. *Review pricing over time.* Ensure that variables such as competitive offerings or costs have not changed enough to impact the price—the "4th C", change, is critical to ensuring appropriate pricing for a product over time.

4. *Don't underestimate the power of the brand.* The premium brand earns the premium price as well. Branding is a subjective issue and only good market research can validate brand recognition and give feedback that a price is the right price.

5. *Keep a holistic pricing approach.* Remember the services, prerequisites and other factors required to use the product successfully. These will also add to the cost of the product in the eyes of customers. Understanding the *Total Cost of Ownership* (TCO) is a great help in pricing a product. TCO takes into consideration all the elements necessary to use a product over its expected life. If possible, compare TCO with the competitions'. This can be a major sales advantage.

6. *Remember that prices can be lowered more easily than raised, but this can send out a very negative message.* Sometimes companies raise prices as a sign of real or supposed success. This tactic is tricky as the value must still be perceived for your product at the new pricing level and must remain positioned appropriately against competition. It is easier to lower prices, but companies that lower prices are sometimes viewed as "in trouble." Additionally, customers who recently purchased the product will likely be upset when they learn that the company just lowered the price for the product. This is why pricing right from the get-go is important with a defendable explanation of the pricing strategy. Often times, prospects will try to negotiate price. Discounting and volume purchases will come into play before the final price is agreed upon between the company and its customers. Keep this in mind when setting the list price.

▪ *Be realistic.* A Product Manager could easily spend all of his or her time on pricing. There is always going to be more data than anyone can analyze to determine the perfect price. Remember that not only is time limited, but things change all the time,

Chapter 9: Going International

Whether starting with an international market strategy or domestic success makes international sales the logical next step, selling software beyond domestic borders is far from a trivial endeavor. For starters, language affects not only how one must communicate with the people who will sell and market the product, it can dramatically alter the way the product works and how it addresses user requirements. In addition, when selling internationally, account for import and export laws, cultural issues, channel considerations and, if selling direct, the overall set-up and accounting for a non-domestic operation, including staffing and labor laws.

Key Questions Before Going Abroad

Before deciding to go international, consider the following:

- What evidence is there that the product is needed in other markets? Is there a business plan that can show distinct revenue? Is the ROI higher than taking on other projects or entering other vertical markets domestically?
- What distribution channels exist for this type of product? Will it be offered in stores, mail order, the Web, local distributors, or through trading partners?
- Are other similar products already offered in the target locales? If not, why not? If so, who are they and what market share do they have? Outside of the domestic market, the competition can be vastly different in terms of players and market leaders.
- Who will be purchasing the product? Will they have the financial means to purchase the product?
- Does the product fit in culturally? Does it fit in with current

business practices? Will there be any laws or governmental influences in how the product is built, sold or used?

- Is a completely localized version of the product needed or do only parts need to be converted? Will the foreign market accept an English version? What is the window of opportunity to get a localized product to market?
- What language versions are needed to start? Is there a rollout plan for the timing of each language needed?

The most common way to get these answers and the quickest, easiest way to get into the local market is by partnering with a local distributor. A good distributor will know the answers to the above questions and if they see significant opportunity, they will usually be of great assistance. Most distributors will serve as a local operation and manage sales, marketing, installation, and customer support. The distributor may assist with or even pay for localization of the product. Using a distributor frees the company from dealing with a host of business, cultural, and language issues that the company on its own will probably not be equipped to deal with. Most companies looking to sell abroad will opt to start with this distributor model and over time, may decide to develop their own local operation. Some of the largest software companies still opt to retain distributors in many of the international markets they serve.

Once it has been confirmed that there is a market opportunity to pursue, get the product ready to be used in different locales. The first step is to understand the difference between internationalization, localization, and globalization, and the implications of doing one without the other. As with all software development, good planning in the beginning can save untold hours and dollars later on when things need to be corrected.

Internationalization

Internationalization is the process of making the software capable of handling multiple languages, including the ability to display and manipulate foreign character sets, grammar, numbers, and dates. Internationalization affects the software, user interface, documentation, error messages, and help files. Essentially, when a product is internationalized, it is not built for a specific language version, but rather it is engineered to easily support different language versions. For example, if the help files and error messages are hard coded into the software itself, it will be much harder to do a translation and insert the new language into the system. Using template or resource files and other smart development techniques can make a huge difference in the effort to create multiple language versions.

Some languages have unique marks such as accents or umlauts. The software must know what to do with these marks and represent them correctly to the user. Often these additional marks are used in conjunction with letters so that they are not necessarily handled like a unique letter themselves. This affects the way letters and words are sorted, alphabetized, associated, and parsed. Special characters can effect the entire application, from the actual processing to the way the file system or database stores and manages data.

Once the product is internationalized, other organizations can do localization. In this way, internal engineers are not needed to create the local language versions of the product (although there may be market-specific features needed which may be isolated for that version only). Having an internationalized version of the master code base can make the delivery process much easier.

One major concern when internationalizing a software product is providing double byte support. Unlike Latin I letters that only require a single computer memory space or "byte" to represent them, other character sets such as Kanji and Farsi may require double the space or "double byte" support. Some languages read left to right, others such as Arabic, right to left, and yet others bottom to top. Fonts and screen size may impact the display of different languages, and many languages have unique rules that depend on context that determines how we sort, alphabetize and associate letters and words.

Today, the most common practice is to provide multi-byte

(UTF-8) support in addition to double-byte UCS2 support. This provides backward compatibility with ASCII. Because internationalization processes and available technologies are frequently enhanced, stay abreast of standards and developments through organizations such as LISA (Localisation Industry Standards Association, www.lisa.org) and others. Most modern development languages such as Java already support double byte and other internationalization requirements.

Differences in measurements (inches versus centimeters), as well as differences in time and date formats must also be accommodated. For example, if the application depends on the system clock or calendaring software, remember holidays and how this relates to other applications and systems with which the software product interacts. Supporting such flexibility in the software may not be a trivial change to the existing product. When designing the product from the get-go, these are some of the important things to consider. Good development practices will ensure that such flexibility is built in and allows the software to behave differently depending on language and context.

Another key consideration in the process of internationalization is specialized hardware and related software needed to support the system. For example, computer keyboards are different in different countries and need to be mapped to the application. Ensure that if there are hardware and software products that are required to run the product (such as compilers, operating systems, and databases), that they are available in the target countries and that these other products are also localized.

Expert consultants, companies and books are available to guide companies on a technical level when engineering a product to be internationalized—from how to form strings to how to design the user interface so that it leaves ample room for different-length questions and answers.

Testing of local versions, including related third party products, should occur in parallel with baseline product development. Extensive testing should be conducted with local people directly in their environment.

Every company that wishes to sell in foreign markets should set up internationalization standards for all products and hold design reviews to ensure conformance. Add internationalization milestones to the product delivery checklist. Quality assurance process should include checks for internationalization standards conformance. Moreover, have a specific group to focus on internationalization initiatives. This committee should identify the goals, tasks and standards needed to make the company more international in its day-to-day practices. (If there is a separate internationalization committee, be sure they are represented at the PDT!).These investments will allow localized products to be delivered faster towards the goal of releasing them simultaneously to multiple markets.

However, this approach may not be realistic for a smaller organization since resources are always tight. In these cases outsourcing to specialized internationalization firms can be attractive. While outsource partners will require a good amount of support from internal engineers, it is still far less effort than if the engineers do the internationalization work themselves. These firms know many tricks of the trade to internationalize a product with minimal pain and risk. However, as with any business partnership, due diligence on the firm is always in order.

Most internationalization outsourcing companies will start the process by doing an assessment to determine the scope of work. Some may charge for the assessment work. At this point, decide whether it makes sense to use internal engineers to implement the recommendations. If the consulting company will implement the changes, they often will absorb the cost of the assessment as part of the overall project.

Every project is different, so it is difficult to provide any rules of thumb for cost or time that an average internationalization project requires. It is rare to skip internationalization and do a local version first unless is for test marketing only one market and the company doesn't have the resources to deal with proper internationalization. By deferring the overall internationalization effort, it might be necessary in the future to formally internationalize the product. This usually means that the work done for the single local version is wasted and will be replaced to accommodate the new international code base.

If the entire effort is outsourced, an internal project leader is needed to manage the project and assist both sides in getting the job done efficiently. The outsource company will need files, documents, and general information to do their job. The outsourcer may do an initial in-depth survey that will need to be coordinated by the project manager. At the same time, ensure that engineers and other product development personnel are involved with the effort so they can integrate the new code and practices into the process.

One vital issue that needs to be managed with the outsourcer is the exchange of source code. The outsourcer may be able to do the work without compiling the final product. Whatever approach is taken, non-disclosure agreements and other documents must be in place to ensure that the company's confidentiality and trade secrets are maintained.

Localization

Localization is the process of creating a specific version of the product to address a target segment's unique requirements and specific language including multiple versions of a given language— American English is different than British English (e.g. "localization" in American English versus "localisation" in British English!). Brazilian Portuguese is different from Portuguese spoken in Portugal. Along with the language differences, various locales represent differences in culture, laws, practices and even voltage.

You should carefully consider what needs to be localized. Many times products can be used in English as long as the documentation is written in local language. You should work with your international channel partners to find out what the minimal requirements are.

Converting the user interface to support the local language will include the words, menu selections, and tool bars. There may be other elements in the software such as graphics or references that need to be localized as well. Help files, documentation, error messages, and installation procedures all need to be converted. Use a distributor or outsource the work to a company with expert translators, especially those that use local people for the process. It is also essential that an expert in the target language (preferably based in the target locale) be the final reviewer. It's usually more cost effective to do the localization abroad. For example, China-based Chinese translators are much less expensive to use than US-based ones. This tends to be true for many countries but not all, so discuss this with the localization partner.

It is important to run local beta tests to ensure that all code executes properly and that all localization changes are accurate and working properly. Be sure to test the user interface, the international characters and formats, the installation and all interoperability with other products that will be co-resident or network accessible.

If the product is internationalized properly, there are ways to estimate the cost for each localization project. Work can be calculated based on the number of words and a unique multiplier or factor for each different language. Many companies, once they get through the first local language version, will have minimal drag time between a new English version and the localized versions. A four-month difference in releases is considered to be "simultaneous release." While it will take much more time the first time out, determine the optimum and realistic time desired between the domestic release and foreign releases. Building synchronization into the internationalization and localization process is critical. Reviewing each release cycle and implementing continuous improvements will assist in reaching the goal.

Globalization

The term "globalization" is often interchanged with internationalization. Some people, however, separate the two terms to identify issues outside of the coding of the software needed to make a product successful in other markets. Globalization is used to describe the processes of establishing the distribution, marketing, sales and support of the product outside of the domestic market. Essentially, globalization considers the infrastructure needed to support doing business internationally.

Distribution

Using a local distributor is often the first choice for entering a local market quickly and with minimal risk by using the distributor's knowledge, local connections and brand. When working with an established distributor, evaluate the other businesses they represent and the customers that they already serve. If the product is shrink-wrapped, what stores will the distributor be able to get the product into? Will the distributor assist in local packaging and production of the software and documentation? Will they provide customer support? If the product is not for mass-consumption, will the distributor do the installation and provide post-sales support and services?

A good distributor will work hard to specify necessary changes and possibly even make the necessary changes to the product to support the local market. It is in their best interest to have the product well integrated to ensure customer satisfaction.

When transferring knowledge to the new distributor, recognize that marketing and training materials are usually first provided in the domestic market language, which is probably not the audience's native tongue. Imagine learning something new and technical - and then imagine learning it in a foreign language. That isn't easy. When presenting information verbally to a foreign audience, speak slowly and don't use difficult words. Leave ample time for questions and if possible, provide a translator, if only for the purpose of helping the audience ask questions. It is usually easier for people to listen and understand information in another language than speaking it themselves. Having the courage to ask a question in a foreign language is often terrifying. In some cultures, it may not be considered appropriate to ask questions in a crowd. Provide a way for the audience to ask questions afterwards in private or via email. Provide as much written information as possible. This allows the students to reinforce the words and it gives them more time to process the ideas. Pictures are very helpful. As with any audience, try to get as much information ahead of time as possible. Are they technical? What other technologies are they familiar with? Have they sold something similar in the past? Again, depending on the culture and the type of job, they may or may not want all the technical details. It may be hard to get accurate feedback from an audience who is being culturally polite. Be sure to follow up with the distributor or other local allies to ensure the information was well transmitted and received.

When operating directly in another country instead of using a distributor, consider the same issues, but additionally, there are issues such as staffing and managing a new, remote organization.

Marketing

The distributor should be able to help promote the product and identify an agency to help do public relations. Using local resources to do PR is critical. A distributor will know the local magazines, analysts and industry movers to go after. A distributor's marketing people can discuss the effectiveness of advertising and the costs in their market, and advise on unique advertising laws. Ask the distributor to do a competitive assessment to get an idea of what and how others are using advertising and other forms of marketing.

In addition to the software, localize the marketing materials and collateral, using native speakers for the translations and final edits. With technical terms and business jargon, it is especially important to have someone who can point out where things "don't quite translate" as intended. For example, Mr. White should not be translated to Sr. Blanco. You will most likely also need to re-do graphics and screenshots. Produce the new print materials on appropriately sized paper such as the European standard A4. And don't forget about the Web site. Create local language versions, local contacts and note local resources.

Be careful about the naming, design and colors used in product packaging and branding. There are endless stories about product names, symbols and logos that are offensive when translated into different languages and cultures. Be sure to run these things by the local representative. It may happen that a local competitor may use similar colors or naming. Also understand the effects of loyalty to locally offered products where another product commands a distinct advantage simply because it's made by a local company.

Sales

When deciding to enter a new international market, spend a lot of up-front time with local colleagues. The Product Manager needs to understand implications of how the product will be marketed, sold, and used. For example, an application that manages customer information should obey the local laws on privacy. Business software such as accounting packages and control systems should conform to the local rules and laws. Understanding the sales process in terms of what tools will be needed and how the cycle works will be invaluable as demos and other collateral are created to assist the local efforts.

Support

Customer support will be a major determinate of success in each foreign locale. Will the corporate support center be used or will the distributor provide customer support? Important issues to consider for support are:

- Will new telephone numbers be needed to support the non-domestic customers? Because 800 numbers do not work outside of North America, will they have a local number to call?

- What about time differences? When can customers contact the support center?
- Will the local language be spoken at the call centers? For example, will the Swiss center have German and French speakers?
- How will issues be tracked and communicated back to corporate? What is the process for escalating issues to appropriate resources? How will a company communicate out to the international local support groups about fixes or other product issues?
- Will corporate provide self-service Web resources and other information in local languages?

Going international is not a trivial undertaking and it requires specialized assistance and strong relationships with distributors. Competing in international markets can be a means of survival, competitiveness, and overall financial success, but first weigh the benefits against the effort and risk before jumping in. Bon voyage!

Appendices

All forthcoming templates are provided as a starting point from which to work on a company's own specific documents and agreements. All legal documents should be reviewed by a professional attorney and are provided here as a means of sample only. The publisher and author are not liable for any issues arising from the use of these templates and stress the importance of customizing them to fit an organization's specific needs and legal requirements.

All templates are available electronically. See page 195 for order information.

Appendix A:
Sample
Base Level Integration Plan

Base Level Integration Plan
Base Level X

Document version: X.X
Date:

Sign Offs:

_____   _____
President/CEO   VP Engineering

_____   _____
VP Marketing   Product Manager

_____   _____
VP Services   VP Sales

Introduction

This is a plan for the development and delivery of the Base Level Integration Plan (BLIP) for *Your Company* software development projects.

This plan consists of two parts. Section one describes the Base Level development process itself. This enables all to review it regularly and new employees to become familiar with it. Section two describes the overall plans of this base level as well as the specific plans of each of the project teams for this specific Base Level (BL).

Your Base Level Integration Process

Process Review

It is important to continuously improve the development process and to do this, a description of the current process is included in each development plan. Each Base Level (BL) or development cycle represents an opportunity to clarify and refine parts of the process that were unclear or problematic in the previous base level(s).

Definitions
(Note important definitions that will be used in describing the process.)

Process Description
(Describe exactly how your process will work. Specify timeframes and activities.)

Base Level "n" Plan

Summary of work to be done:
(Describe the overall features or other enhancements to be done for this release)

Assumptions

The following general assumptions are being made:

(Note any important assumptions about resources or other dependencies required to carry out the plan.)

Summary of Projects

First Requirement to be Addressed:

    Summary of requirement and work to be completed:

    Project Leader:

      Project Task Team:
      (note hours or percentage of time to be used from each member)

    Tasks include:

    Total Estimated Project Time:

Second Requirement to be Addressed

    Summary of requirement and work to be completed:

    Project Leader:

      Project Task Team: *(note hours or percentage of time to be used from each member)*

    Tasks include:

Total Estimated Project Time:

(Continue list for all requirements that will be met during this Base Level)

Costs
(Note cost of human resources in development, documentation and QA group needed to work on this BL.)

Costs in addition to engineering manpower may include:
(Note any software, hardware, consulting, etc. needed to complete tasks)

BL*n* Schedule
(Sample 27 week cycle total, 12 week implementation phase)

	Base Level n	Base Level n+1
Requirements Phase	Jan 1 – Jan 15 (2 weeks)	April 11 – April 24 (2 weeks)
Planning Phase	Jan 16 – Jan 29 (2 weeks)	April 25 – May 8 (2 weeks)
Implementation Phase	Jan 30 – April 24 (12 weeks)	May 8 – July 31 (12 weeks)
Integration Phase	April 25 – May 8 (2 weeks)	Aug 1 – Aug 14 (2 weeks)
Alpha Period	May 9 – May 15 (1 week)	Aug 15 – Aug 21 (1 week)
Beta Period	May 15 – July 10 (8 weeks)	Aug 21 – Oct 16 (8 weeks)
GA Release	July 11	Oct 17

Main Risks
(Note any real issues that may affect the organization's ability to deliver the planned functionality.)

Key Resource Constraints
(Note any people, hardware or other resources that are limited or necessary for the completion of the work.)

Quality Assurance Plan

The major tasks for BLn QA include:

Project Members:

Resources Required:

Appendix B: Sample Requirements Document

Requirement ID Number	Date Entered	Priority (High, Med, Low)	Functional Description	Source	Status	Estimated Revenue Opportunity	Estimated Development Hours	ROI = Revenue - (Hours * hourly expense)
1.00	3/18/02	High	Port Admin tools to Windows NT V4.0	Customer X	Planned for this BLIP cycle	Will help reduce maintenance of separate platform tools required	20	NA
2.00	5/18/01	Med	Improve performance by at least 2X	Engineering	In consideration	$5,000	25	$1,875
3.00	5/2/02	High	Allow users to customize screens (see detailed description document for more information)	Support	Hold for future consideration	$100,000	30	$96,250
3.01	5/10/01	Low	Change background color on all screens to green	Jerry in sales	For future consideration	TBD	TBD	TBD

Appendix C:
Sample
Non-Disclosure Agreement

This Confidentiality Agreement ("Agreement") is entered into as of the ___ day of _____, 2002, by and between (your company), a (*name state of incorporation*) corporation with its principal place of business at (*your company's address*) ("*abbreviation if any for your company name*") and

_____, a _____

corporation with its principal place of business at

_____

("Company").

1. This Agreement shall apply to all confidential and proprietary information disclosed by the parties to each other, including, without limitation, all mailing lists, proprietary data, data model(s), data integrators, product designs, capabilities, specifications, program code, software systems and processes, information regarding existing and future technical, business and marketing plans and product strategies and the identity of actual and potential customers, data providers and suppliers (hereinafter referred to as "Confidential Information"). Confidential Information shall also include the proprietary information of either party's subsidiaries, affiliated companies, business partners, data providers and clients. Confidential Information may be written, oral, recorded, or contained on tape or on other electronic or mechanical media.

2. "Confidential Information" shall not include information which (a) was already known to the receiving party prior to the time that it is disclosed to such party hereunder; (b) is in or has entered the public domain through no breach of this Agreement or other wrongful act of the receiving party; (c) has been rightfully received from a third party without breach of this Agreement; (d) has been approved for release by written authorization of the disclosing party; or (e) is required to be disclosed pursuant to the final binding order of a governmental agency or court of

competent jurisdiction, provided that the disclosing party has been given reasonable notice of the pendency of such an order and the opportunity to contest it.

3. Each party agrees to hold the other's Confidential Information in strict trust and confidence and not to disclose such Confidential Information to any third party or to use it for any purpose other than as specifically authorized by the other party. Each party agrees that it will employ all reasonable steps to protect the Confidential Information of the other party from unauthorized or inadvertent disclosure, including without limitation all steps that it takes to protect its own information that it considers proprietary. The parties may disclose each other's Confidential Information only to those employees having a need to know and only to the extent necessary to enable the parties to adequately perform their respective responsibilities to each other. The parties hereby undertake to ensure the individual compliance of such employees with the terms hereof.

4. No copies of the Confidential Information shall be made by the receiving party except as may be necessary to perform services relating to the Confidential Information as requested by the disclosing party. Upon the written request of the disclosing party at any time, the receiving party shall, at the disclosing party's option, either destroy or return to the disclosing party all tapes, diskettes or other media upon which the disclosing party's Confidential Information is stored, and all copies thereof, if any. If requested by the disclosing party to destroy any Confidential Information, the receiving party shall certify in a writing to be delivered to the disclosing party within five (5) business days following such destruction that such destruction has been completed.

5. Each party shall be deemed to be the owner of all Confidential

Information disclosed by it hereunder, including all patent, copyright, mask work, trademark, service mark, trade secret and any and all other proprietary rights and interests therein, and *(your company)* and Company each agree that nothing contained in this Agreement shall be construed as granting any rights, by license or otherwise, in or to any Confidential Information disclosed pursuant to this Agreement.

6. The parties acknowledge that the unauthorized disclosure, use or disposition of Confidential Information could cause irreparable harm and significant injury that may be difficult to ascertain. Accordingly, the parties agree that the disclosing party shall have the right to an immediate injunction without bond in the event of any breach of this Agreement, in addition to any other remedies that may be available to the disclosing party at law or in equity.

7. The parties acknowledge that they are aware that the federal securities laws prohibit any person who has material, non-public information concerning a publicly traded company such as *(your company)* from purchasing or selling the securities of such company, or from communicating such material, non-public information to any other person if it is reasonably foreseeable that such other person is likely to purchase or sell the securities of such company. The parties therefore agree to refrain from engaging in activities that would violate such federal securities laws. *(note: this section may not apply to every company.)*

8. If any provision of this Agreement or any portion of any such provision shall be held invalid or unenforceable by a court of competent jurisdiction, the remaining provisions of this Agreement shall remain in full force and effect, and the provision or portion thereof affected by such holding shall be modified, if possible, so that it is enforceable to the maximum extent permissible.

9. This Agreement shall continue until terminated in writing by either party; provided, however, that the obligation to protect the confidentiality of all Confidential Information disclosed by the parties to each other prior to such termination shall survive the termination of the Agreement.

10. This Agreement shall not be terminated or superseded by any future agreement between the parties hereto, unless such subsequent agreement specifically so provides by an express reference to this Agreement.

10. This Agreement shall be governed by and construed in accordance with the laws of the Commonwealth of *(your company's state)*, without regard to conflict of law principles, and shall benefit and be binding upon the parties hereto and their respective successors and assigns.

IN WITNESS WHEREOF, the parties hereto have caused this Agreement to be executed by its duly authorized representatives as of the date first written above.

Your Company   *Company X*

BY:_____   BY: _____
    (Signature)   (Signature)

_____   _____
(Print or Type Name)   (Print or Type Name)

_____   _____
    (Title)   (Title)

Appendix D:
Sample
PDT Rules of Engagement

PDT Objective:

To identify and resolve cross-functional product delivery issues.

Rules of Engagement:

1. All members of the PDT have equal say and opinions. In cases where a member cannot agree on an issue, the PDT Leader will act as the judge and make the final decision.
2. All members are obligated to bring forward issues that are pertinent to the topic being discussed. It will be unacceptable for people to leave PDT saying that they weren't heard or that their issue was not addressed.
3. All members will conduct themselves professionally with respect for their fellow members and departments.
4. Any issue that is specific to a department or person that is related to non-performance will be addressed outside of the meeting.
5. The PDT meeting leader will have the right to manage the meeting and table discussions if necessary for outside or later follow up. All members have the obligation to contribute to this action if they feel the discussion is inappropriate or unnecessary in PDT.
6. All members will come prepared for the meeting having reviewed the agenda and knowing what they are expected to discuss. Each member must come prepared having reviewed his or her department checklist and represent their readiness at the meeting each time. If a member cannot make the meeting, it is imperative that a substitute is sent that can voice and vote in the member's absence. Absenteeism will not be an acceptable excuse for being ignorant of current status
7. Minutes have continued to be published soon after the meeting. All members are obligated to review them and report any missing or incorrect information to the PDT

Leader immediately. Any questions stemming from the minutes should be raised immediately as well. Members are responsible for sharing the minutes and relevant issues with his or her departmental colleagues.

8. PDT is not a substitute for day-to-day cross-functional communication. It is stressed that PDT can not be all things to everyone but should function as a way for all parties to stay abreast of critical issues as they may pertain to each function.

9. Issues with the meetings themselves should be reported to the PDT Leader directly so that we can continue to improve the process.

10. PDT issues inevitably will raise the question of certain department(s) performance and the way things are currently being handled in order to improve such process. This should not be taken as an insult to anyone in particular. As noted above, specific performance issues with individuals should be addressed outside of PDT, however, as would be expected, in order to fix some things, we must identify where things are not working currently. These discussions should remain department-level and not be taken personally.

Appendix E:
Sample PDT Checklist

ACTION/TASK	RESPONSIBLE DEPT	OUTPUT	SIGN OFF	DATE/STATUS
Requirements Phase				Jan 2 - Jan 20
Ongoing product requirement input	Product Management	Requirements Document	Product Management	Done
Review/evaluate core dependent/independent partner requirements	Product Management	Product Requirements doc	Partner Marketing	Done
Submit requirements for current Base Level	Product Management	Current Base Level Requirements Document	Engineering	Done
Planning Phase				Jan 21 - Jan 31
Do initial scoping of high requirements	Engineering	Initial scoping meeting with Product Management	Engineering	Done
Conduct ROI analysis on current requirements	Product Management	ROI inputs into Requirements Document	Finance	Done
Finalize requirements for current Base Level	Product Management	Final document with ROI and priorities	PDT	Done
Review requirements doc for new features in BL	Professional Services	Understand impact of new features for implementation	Professional Services	Done
Develop BL Plan	Engineering	BL Plan Document	PDT	In progress
Review any contractual responsibilities with partners/vendors	Finance	Payment schedule of any royalty, annual maintenance, or license fee for product/service	Channel Sales/Partner Marketing	Done

Alpha Testing Phase				Mar 14-Mar 31
BL Knowledge Transfer	Documentation/QA	New product feature awareness	Professional Services	
Knowledge Transfer Doc hand-off	Documentation/QA	Complete documentation of new features	Professional Services	
Receive baseline code for alpha testing	Engineering	Unchanged code for alpha testing	Professional Services	
Review weekly alpha results	Engineering/Prod Mgmt	Problem reports & suggestions	Engineering	
Generate PDF user guides from source files	Documentation	Set of PDF user guides	Documentation	
Generate online Help from source files	Documentation	Online Help sets	Documentation	
Beta Testing Phase				Mar 31- May 14
Select Beta Users	Product Management	Customer beta sites	Product Management	
Beta Release	Engineering	Customer ready beta code	Professional Services	
Install beta sites	Professional Services	Beta site installed for testing	Professional Services	
Train channel partner on new BL features	Product Management	Product positioning & awareness	Partner Marketing	
Train beta sites	Product Management	Beta site trained for testing	Product Management	
Review weekly beta report with customer feedback	Product Management	Problem reports & suggestions	Engineering	
Develop/review/draft marketing collateral	Marketing	Draft collateral for new product	Product Management	

General Availability Phase				15-May
Final code delivered	Engineering	Generally available product	Professional Services	
Product Announcement to Channel Sales/Partners	Product Management	Coordinate rollout plan with partner(s) including joint internal/external announcement including updated collateral, demos, proposals	Partner Marketing	
Send and post press release	Marketing	Distribute press release on new version with user quotes	Marketing	
Article in Customer Newsletter about new version	Marketing/Product Mgmt	Customer awareness of new product functionality	Sales	
Article in Partner Newsletter on new version	Marketing	Partner awareness of new product functionality	Channel Sales/Partner Marketing	
Quarterly webcast to review new version with customers/partners	Product Management	Regular webcast to discuss what's new	Sales/Channel Sales	

Appendix F:
Sample Product Business Plan

Product Name

Product Release
Document version #
Date

Revision History

This should discuss the changes made to this document itself as it is updated and distributed. Note the date and document revision number and a brief description of the changes made.

Legal Name of Product

Note the name of the product and any trademarks. Be clear on any specific branding such as capital letters or other style requirements. Include a logo if appropriate and specifications on color (PMS and process palette), font and size details.

Purpose of Product

Briefly describe what the product does and why would someone would purchase it.

Target Market

Describe the target market. Be as quantitative as possible. Who will use it and why are they more likely than other markets?

What Can the Product Do?

List the main features of the product and what benefits they provide for a user.

Current Available Release

List the current release version and new features added.

Product Lineage

List previous versions of the product and main features added at each release. Include dates of release.

Platform Availability

What hardware, software and networks are supported? (Be as specific as possible) Note if the solution is to be a hosted solution.

Sales Channels

Identify who is selling the product and what is their strategy (i.e. direct to end users, indirect via resellers, etc.). Note any geographic limitations or advantages.

Target Volume

Provide forecasts information on how many will be sold and by which distribution channel.

Customer Training Available

List what classes or other training resources are available for customers on the product in general and this new release.

Internal Training Plans

Describe who and how your internal staff will be trained on the new product. Include all functions, even if some are not applicable.

Internal Training Resources

List what resources (people, documents, CBTs, etc) are available for other employees, partners and consultants to gain product information.

Services Available

Describe what services (installation, consulting, etc.) are available to support the product.

Product Support Plan

Describe how the product will be supported (via telephone, email, web chat, etc.). What materials does the support staff need to provide service?

Product Documentation Available

Note what kind of user documentation is available (context sensitive help or other online support) and on what media (CD, hardcopy, etc.)

Configuration Information

Describe pre-requisite hardware and software as well as hardware sizing requirements (memory, disk, etc.). Note any specific issues for customers who may be upgrading to the new version.

Product Contents/Bill of Materials

If product is composed of sub-components, describe this.

Pricing

List the product price and the price for any related products and services. If this is an upgrade, note whether it is chargeable to existing customers or not. Also note any upgrade requirements in terms of pre-requisite software that must be purchased or upgraded.

Order Information

Describe how to order the product. Include any product code and contract information that is required to fulfill an order.

Additional Options/Add-on's

Describe any other products or services that should be considered with the purchase of this product.

Distribution Process

Briefly describe the distribution process. Once an order is placed, how does it get fulfilled?

Available Media

Note which media the product available on (CD, FTP, tape, disks, etc.).

Physical Packaging

Describe how the product will be packaged. Ideally include pictures for the various components.

Royalties

Note any royalties due with the sale of the product.

Announcement Plans

Describe the announcement plans for the product including press releases, internal announcements and other marketing promotions.

Marketing Collateral

List available marketing collateral for the product.

Competitive Information

Summarize the competition and refer to other sources of competitive information.

Product Financials

Include product financial analysis on forecasted revenues and expected expenses. Show breakeven and overall ROI.

Appendix G:
Sample Beta Test Plan

Beta Test Plan

Beta Site Company Name: _____

Contact Name: _____

Contact Information: Phone: _____
                            Email: _____
                            Address: _____
                            _____

Date: _____

Product to be Beta Tested: _____

Version of Product:_____

This Beta Test Site Project Plan is provided to assist you in preparing your beta test plan. As you fill out this plan, please keep in mind that the more information you can provide on your testing, the better. All information is vitally important to our successful launch of our new product. Your time and effort in completing this information and providing us the opportunity to work with you on this beta testing is greatly appreciated.

Overview

This document describes the testing that will be performed by Beta Test Participants for * YOUR COMPANY products (hereafter referred to as "Tester(s)") to verify the functionality and quality of *YOUR COMPANY software. Beta Testing is done to ascertain from a third party's perspective whether the product is ready for general use and sale.

The purpose of this beta test project plan is to ensure that the Tester has the necessary information needed to successfully test the new product. Therefore, we ask you to fill this in with as many details as possible. This information really does help expedite the beta testing process and in the end, helps all of us get the product out sooner with better quality.

In addition to this document, all test site candidates will be asked to sign a beta test agreement to ensure that both companies legally acknowledge the beta level of the software being used and that neither shall hold each other liable for issues arising out of the use of this pre-released software.

As the Tester completes the beta testing, *YOUR COMPANY will request a final beta test summary to be submitted using the short template that will be supplied by *YOUR COMPANY. This summary describes what was tested, the problems that were found and the resolutions to those problems. Finally, it also asks the tester to sign off on the product's release as verification of a third party endorsement of its quality within the testing boundaries of that particular test or set of tests. Products without final test summaries will not be released until sufficient beta evidence is provided.

*YOUR COMPANY will deliver updates to beta release software on a regular basis and contact the beta site representative when this is available.

*Support for the beta test will be handled by *YOUR COMPANY Customer Care/Support, please identify yourself as a beta test site for this product. All support issues and custom patch requests for the test software should be directed to Customer Care, where they will be routed to the appropriate Engineering or* *support contact.*

We thank you for your participation in this beta test program and look forward to a mutually fulfilling experience.

YOUR COMPANY

Overview of Project

Please briefly describe how you will be using *YOUR COMPANY* beta software, including specific project objectives.

_____

_____

_____

_____

_____

* YOUR COMPANY's **Testing Objectives:**

The following is *YOUR COMPANY 's list of objectives for the

beta testing. This should be an all-inclusive list of the features of the

product. *YOUR COMPANY is requesting the beta testers to create

different scenarios using all the product features. Please provide *

YOUR COMPANY with copies of your beta testing documentation

of the criteria used for each objective in order for us to verify

thorough product testing was completed.

(Product Management will provide List of objectives per product)

What features of the beta software do you intend to exercise?

_____

_____

_____

_____

_____

_____

_____

_____

What are your expectations from this software and from this test?

_____

_____

_____

_____

_____

How many people will be working on the test? What are their names and titles? What are the man-hours assigned? (E.g., George Smith, Marketing Rep, 50%)

_____

_____

_____

_____

_____

_____

_____

What is your testing timeline?

What are the significant milestones?

_____

_____

_____

_____

_____

_____

_____

_____

Appendix H:
Sample
Beta License Agreement

(* Note: there are several places where you will need to note your company's name or state of incorporation or the name of your beta site. These places are noted as *)

Subject to the provisions contained herein, * *Your Company*. ("Licensor") hereby grants to ** Your Beta Site*   ("Licensee") a nonexclusive, restricted license to use its proprietary computer software product ("Software") solely for the purpose of evaluating and testing the Software during the "Beta Period", as solely defined by Licensor and communicated to Licensee.

SOFTWARE AND DOCUMENTATION. Licensor shall furnish the Software listed below to Licensee in machine-readable object code form and provide **Your Company's Name* documentation for operation and use of the Software ("Documentation"). Licensor shall provide Licensee with a password that enables the Software to be used by Licensee during the Beta Period.

LICENSE TERM. The term of this Beta Agreement and the license granted herein commences upon the date of this Agreement and ceases upon the end of the "Beta Period" or upon the First Customer Shipment of the Software; which ever comes first. Ownership and Proprietary Information rights and restrictions shall survive termination of this Agreement.

BETA TEST REPORTING. The Licensee agrees to provide timely, and reasonably accurate and complete information regarding the quality and usage of the Software and Documentation during the Beta Period. Licensee shall report malfunctions and bugs directly and only to the Licensor.

TITLE. Title and ownership rights in and to the Software and Documentation shall remain exclusively in **Your Company*. The Software is provided for Licensee's own internal use under this license. This license does not include the right to sublicense and is personal to Licensee and therefore may not be assigned (by operation of law or otherwise) or transferred. Licensee acknowledges that the Software source code remains a confidential trade secret of **Your Company* and therefore agrees not to attempt or knowingly allow others to decipher, decompile or reverse engineer the Software or determine how *Your Company* develops passwords.

WARRANTY. Licensee understands the Software and Documentation is of Beta quality, and that there is no warranty with respect to such Software and Documentation. *YOUR COMPANY* DOES NOT WARRANT ANY BETA RELEASE; BETA RELEASES ARE DISTRIBUTED "AS IS." *YOUR COMPANY* MAKES NO EXPRESSED OR IMPLIED WARRANTY AND EXPRESSLY DISCLAIMS ALL WARRANTIES OF MERCHANTABILITY OR FITNESS FOR A PARTICULAR PURPOSE. Additionally, portions of the Software and Documentation may be derived from third-party software and no such third party warrants the Software or Documentation, assumes any liability regarding use of the Software or Documentation, or undertakes to furnish any support or information relating to the Software or Documentation. Licensor explicitly excludes any and all warranties and indemnities related to an Infringement in connection with third party software.

RESTRICTED USE. The Software and Documentation shall be used exclusively by Licensee and Licensee shall not allow others to use or have access to the Software and Documentation, either directly or indirectly. Licensee may not export the Software from the United States (or the Country in which the license has been granted), modify the Software or Documentation, or make derivative or compilation works of them.

LIMITATION OF LIABILITY. Licensee's sole and exclusive remedies for any damage or loss arising out of or in any way connected with the Software or Documentation, shall be, at Licensor's option, repair or replacement of the Software or Documentation, or return or credit of the fees paid (if any) in connection with licensing such Software or Documentation. Under no circumstances and under no legal theory, tort, contract, or otherwise, shall *YOUR COMPANY* be liable to Licensee or any other person for any special, incidental, or consequential damages of any character including, without limitation, damages for loss of good will, loss of data, work stoppage, computer failure or malfunction, or any and all other commercial damages or losses, or for any damages in excess of the fees paid to Licensor for a license to the Software and Documentation, even if Licensor or *YOUR COMPANY* shall have been informed of the possibility thereof.

TERMINATION. Either party may terminate this Agreement at any time with written notification to the other party. Upon termination of this Agreement, Licensee shall immediately discontinue the use of the Software and shall within ten days return to Licensor all copies of the Software and Documentation.

PROPRIETARY INFORMATION. Licensee shall keep in trust and confidence all Proprietary Information. Proprietary Information means all data, information, know-how, programs or intelligence, whether in machine readable or visually readable form, which is the property of and is confidential and proprietary to *YOUR COMPANY*, or which is derived from such confidential information. Licensee specifically acknowledges that all forms of the Beta Software and Documentation are considered Proprietary and Confidential Information. Licensee also acknowledges that all information it develops or acquires relating to the Beta Software and Documentation shall also be considered Confidential Information until the Information is released for general distribution.

RESOLUTION OF DISPUTES. Any claim of whatever nature including but not limited to the issue of dispute resolution arising out of or relating to the Agreement shall be resolved pursuant to the dispute resolution procedure as follows: If any disputes are not resolved by informal negotiations of the parties, then the parties agree to submit to non-binding mediation in accordance with the Mediation Rules of the American Arbitration Association (the "AAA"); and In the event the parties are unable to resolve issues by using mediation, then the parties shall have all rights available to them at law or in equity.

MISCELLANEOUS. This Agreement represents the complete and exclusive statement of the agreements concerning this license between the parties and supersedes all prior agreements and representations between them. It may be amended only by a writing executed by both parties. If any provision of this Agreement is held to be ineffective, unenforceable, or illegal under certain circumstances for any reason, such decision shall not affect e validity or enforceability (i) of such provision under other circumstances or (ii) of the remaining provisions hereof under all circumstances and such provision shall be reformed to and only to the extent necessary to make it effective, enforceable and legal under such circumstances. All headings are solely for convenience and shall not be considered in interpreting this Agreement. This Agreement shall be governed by and construed under *The state where your company is incorporated law as such law applies to agreements between *The state where your company is incorporate] residents entered into and to be performed entirely within *The state where your company is incorporate] except as required by U.S. Government rules and regulations to be governed by Federal Law.

Beta Software: _____

_____

_____

Beta Period Start-Date: _____**Beta Period End-Date**: _____

LICENSEE: _____   **LICENSOR:**

Signature: _____   Signature: _____

Name: _____   Name: _____

Title: _____   Title: _____

Date: _____   Date: _____

Appendix I:
Sample
Beta Test Summary Report

Beta Site Company Name: _____

Contact Name: _____

Contact Information: Phone: _____
                              Email: _____
                              Address: _____

                              _____

 Date: _____

Product that was in Beta Test: _____
Version of Product: _____

Please complete the following to the best of your ability. We cannot release this product without evidence that complete beta testing has been done. It is therefore very important to *Your Company and anyone desiring the final version of the product that this information be shared with *Your Company as soon as possible. Your name, test results and system information is Proprietary and Confidential information and will be kept in confidence.

We appreciate your participation in our Beta Test and hope that you have found the experience worthwhile.

1.   Per my Beta Test Plan, I did complete the expected testing:

Yes _____No____;
              Please explain:

_____

_____

2.   During my Beta Testing, I found the following problems:

_____ Reported? Y ____N ____
                        Resolved? Y ____N ____
_____ Reported? Y ____N ____
                        Resolved? Y ____N ____
_____ Reported? Y ____N ____
                        Resolved? Y ____N ____
_____ Reported? Y ____N ____
                        Resolved? Y ____N ____
_____ Reported? Y ____N ____
                        Resolved? Y ____N ____
_____ Reported? Y ____N ____
                        Resolved? Y ____N ____
_____ Reported? Y ____N ____
                        Resolved? Y ____N ____

3. Problems I believe are unresolved:

_____
_____
_____
_____

4. Please comment on the effectiveness of the documentation you used during this beta test. Any and all input is very much appreciated.

_____
_____
_____
_____

5. Other Comments:

_____
_____

Signed: _____ Date: _____

Suggested Readings

The Product Marketing Handbook for Software, 4th Edition;
by Merrill R. Chapman; Aegis Resources, Inc.; 2004.
www.aegis-resources.com

The Balanced Scorecard : Translating Strategy into Action
by Robert Kaplan S. and David P. Norton, Harvard Business School
Press, 1996.

*The Business of Software: What Every Manager, Programmer,
and Entrepreneur Must Know to Thrive and Survive in Good
Times and Bad*
By Michael A. Cusumano, Free Press, a division of Simon &
Schuster, 2004.

*In Search of Stupidity: Over 20 Years of High-Tech Marketing
Disasters, 2nd edition* by Merrill R. Chapman *www.insearchofstupdity.com*

Marketing Profs provides well written articles, webinars and other
resources on all topics of marketing. Not all content is free and
requires a subscription membership. *http://www.marketingprofs.com/*

Internet Marketing information: Market Vantage Inc.
http://www.market-vantage.com/resources/index.htm

Product Management Resources

National Product Management / Marketing Associations and Forums

Association of International Product Marketing & Management
http://www.aipmm.com/

American Marketing Association's Marketing Power site
http://www.marketingpower.com

Product Development and Management Association
http://www.pdma.org. There are also many local chapters of the PDMA. Check their website for contact information.

Software Product Marketing
http://groups.yahoo.com/group/softwareproductmarketing/

Regional professional groups for PMs and PMMs

(These change often so be sure to do a search in your local area):

Atlanta TechProduct Management Association
http://finance.groups.yahoo.com/group/atpma

Austin Product Marketing & Management
http://finance.groups.yahoo.com/group/AustinPMMForum

Boston Product Management Association
http://www.bostonproducts.org

Portland (OR) Product Marketing Exchange
http://finance.groups.yahoo.com/group/PDX-PME

Raleigh/Durham – Triangle Product Marketing Association
http://finance.groups.yahoo.com/group/trianglepma

San Diego Product Management Association http://www.sdpma.org

Puget Sound Product Management Association
http://finance.groups.yahoo.com/group/PSPM

Silicon Valley Product Management Association
http://www.svpma.org
&
http://finance.groups.yahoo.com/group/
siliconvalleyproductmanagers

Digital Capital Product Management Association (Washington DC)
http://finance.groups.yahoo.com/group/dcpma

Newsletters and articles

The 280 Group offers a newsletter by signing on their website at
www.280group.com. 280 group provides consulting and numerous
toolkits to assist companies with product management.

Daniel Shefer: product management articles
http://shefer.net/articles

Sequent Learning Networks, Inc. offers training, consulting, and a
regular newsletter. Sign up on their website at *www.sequentlearning.com*.

Pragmatic Marketing offers training, consulting, and a newsletter is
designed for Product Managers and Marketing managers, each

newsletter offers observations about Product Management issues facing high-tech firms. To subscribe, send an email to *subscribe@pragmaticmarketing.com* or go to http://www.pragmaticmarketing.com/resources/newsletter.asp.

The Product Management Challenge; weekly newsletter on various Product Management issues. Send email to subscribe: *jacquesm@epix.net?subject=Subscribe*

The Software Marketing newsletter reports trends, technologies, companies and resources for software publishers. *http://www.softwaremarketsolution.com/*

Softletter: The Leading Source of Hard Data about the Business of Software *www.softletter.com*

Index

About the Author

ALYSSA S. DVER has over 20 years of experience in software product management and marketing. She was Chief Marketing Officer for SEDONA Corporation where she helped make the company the leading customer relationship management (CRM) vendor in the banking market. Prior to joining SEDONA, Dver was the founder of Lead Factory Inc., a Web-based lead management solution, where she conceptualized and led the company to develop a patent-pending product, now installed at over 300 banks worldwide. She has executive management experience in companies of all sizes, including Empresa Inc., CenterLine Software, Cincom Systems, and Digital Equipment Corporation. She has held positions with worldwide responsibilities, based domestically as well as overseas.

As a freelance contributor, Ms. Dver has written business and technology articles for publications including BusinessWeek, Forbes, Entrepreneur Magazine, Software Magazine, CRM Magazine and others. She is frequently quoted in the media as a software management expert and is a requested speaker at trade conferences, professional associations, business schools, and customer events. She is also the founder and CEO of Wander Wear Inc., a company dedicated to lost child prevention.

Ms. Dver graduated from the Wharton School, University of Pennsylvania with a major in Marketing.

Appendix Templates
are available online

Save time. Purchase the templates in
Microsoft Word and RTF formats

www.swproductmanagement.com

Your Complete BPM Library

Innovation at the Intersection of Business and Technology

www.mkpress.com